ANANDA COURSE IN SELF-REALIZATION

A Handbook on Discipleship

ANANDA COURSE IN SELF-REALIZATION

A Handbook on Discipleship

Based on the Teachings of Paramhansa Yogananda

Swami Kriyananda

Crystal Clarity Publishers
Nevada City, California

Crystal Clarity Publishers, Nevada City, CA 95959
Copyright © 2010, 1996 by Hansa Trust
First edition 1996. Second edition 2010
All rights reserved. Published 2010

Printed in the USA

ISBN: 978-1-56589-178-4

*Cover photograph and design by Barbara Bingham, produced by Crystal
Clarity Publishers. Interior layout and design by Crystal Clarity Publishers.*

www.crystalclarity.com
800.424.1055
clarity@crystalclarity.com

Contents

Introduction

Someone once asked Swami Kriyananda, "Do I need a guru?"

Those present, knowing of his life-long discipleship to Paramhansa Yogananda, were surprised to hear his response, "No, you don't." He then added, "But if you want to find God, you need a guru."

No one would think twice about seeking an expert guide when climbing a mountain, learning a musical instrument, or becoming a competitive athlete. Yet in attaining spiritual freedom, surely the most difficult endeavor of all, many try to make their own way by cobbling together various beliefs and practices. Often these choices are based on nothing more than personal likes and dislikes.

This *Handbook on Discipleship* explains why a guru is needed, what a true guru is, and how to follow the guru. It also clears up many common misunderstandings on the subject that are prevalent in current spiritual thinking.

These lessons offer a rare opportunity to learn about discipleship from a lifelong disciple of a fully realized Master. Swami Kriyananda has been a disciple of Paramhansa Yogananda for over sixty years. For all of the extraordinary accomplishments of Swami Kriyananda's life—over one hundred books, over four hundred pieces of music, successful spiritual communities all over the world, and more - he gives full credit to Yogananda and to what he has gained as his disciple.

The first part of the book shares teachings that are universal to the Guru-Disciple relationship, even though they are based on the specific relationship of Swami Kriyananda with Paramhansa Yogananda. Some of the subjects covered in the first part include:

- Does one need a *living* guru?
- The role of divine grace in spiritual progress
- How to follow a guru
- How to draw on the guru's power
- The importance of attunement and magnetism

The second part describes the process of becoming a disciple of Paramhansa Yogananda. It includes a Discipleship Initiation Ceremony, which helps to connect the new disciple to the thousands of disciples who are part of *Ananda*—a worldwide movement of people who have been following Yogananda for many decades.

Through these lessons, we hope you will come to know how to draw the grace of the guru into your life, and how to receive it more fully until you become one with God.

Ananda Course in Self-Realization

The Path of Kriya Yoga

Ananda Sangha Worldwide has been spreading the teachings of meditation and yoga for over forty years. Our teachers live the practices that are taught in this book. If you have any questions about the course material, or simply want to talk to someone, we are here to help you.

Ananda Course Support

course@ananda.org
530-470-2340
www.anandacourse.com

14618 Tyler Foote Road, #145
Nevada City, CA 95959

Ananda Kriya Sangha

kriyayoga2@ananda.org
530-478-7624
www.ananda.org

PART ONE

Lessons in Discipleship

Chapter 1

UNDERSTANDING THE
NEED FOR A GURU

Words of Paramhansa Yogananda

People who are still locked up in the cage of ego often view the prospect of having a guru as a threat to their personal freedom. They don't realize that freedom is exactly what they don't have at present!

The guru's role is to open the door of the cage. If a disciple, finding himself still attached to limitation, cries, "Leave me alone; I like my nice little nest of pleasures and desires!" the guru won't insist. He will say, simply, "I came because you called me; otherwise I would not have troubled. It wasn't my need that brought me. It was your need. So, until you call me again, I will wait."

Accepting a guru isn't the assumption of a burden! It isn't a menace to a person's free will and happiness! It is the greatest blessing that you, or anyone, can possibly have in this world. Incarnations of good karma are required to attract the help of a true guru.

God sends the seeker indirect guidance at first, through books and lesser teachers. Only when the desire for Him is very strong does He send help in the form of a Self-realized guru. It is no favor to the guru if the student accepts him. Rather, the student must have prayed very hard, in this lifetime and in former lives, to have earned so great a blessing.

It isn't that you need to go out looking for the guru. The Lord will send him to you, or else draw you to him, when you are spiritually ready.

—*The Essence of Self-Realization: The Wisdom of Paramhansa Yogananda*, by Swami Kriyananda. *See Resources.*

Understanding the Need for a Guru

Taken from Talks by Swami Kriyananda

We are living in an age where the thought of discipleship is not pleasing to most people. It was my own tendency as a young man to be an intellectual rebel. When it came to religion I didn't think that anybody could teach me anything, because, first of all, I assumed that nobody knew anything. Secondly, I thought that finding Truth was something that demanded such integrity on one's own part that to take answers from anyone else would not be staying true to oneself. Finally, I reached the point where I saw that all my efforts to improve myself weren't getting me anywhere. I would be working on one side of my nature trying to improve that, only to find the other side was beginning to deteriorate for lack of sufficient energy.

I recognized also how ignorant I was, and how often things that looked good to me turned out for some strange reason not to work out at all. Though I hadn't even accepted that there was a God, I was desperate to find Truth. That was why, though I thought that I'd never say these words to anyone, the first thing I uttered when I met Paramhansa Yogananda was, "I want to be your disciple." I didn't want it in the sense of being somebody's servant, or of passively turning over the responsibility for my life to somebody else. But I understood that if you wanted to be a good painter, you eventually had to go to somebody who knew his art. If you really wanted to know God, you had to learn from someone who had found Him.

Do We Need a Guru?

Why do we need a guru? Let's put it this way: The dynamo in a city can't be plugged directly into the light circuits of our homes. It would blow out the circuits because it's too powerful. It has to be stepped down by transformers until it's brought to the level of one hundred and twenty volts that our circuits can handle. The same thing is true of our own nervous system and consciousness. Cosmic consciousness is so incredibly beyond our human perceptions and beyond our human capacity to receive that we couldn't handle it. It must be fed to us gradually, and stepped down by transformers. The guru is that transformer for the divine consciousness of God.

Another point is that sometimes in meditation you can feel a touch of the divine power which is overwhelming. It's so immense! It's so inconceivably great that when you are in touch with that power aspect of God, you feel as if you could be snuffed out and it wouldn't even be noticed. It isn't true, but you feel that this power is so immense that nothing you are could possibly signify anything in comparison. It's a state that the ego isn't readily prepared to accept. So it is that we need to grow gradually into this expansion of awareness. We need to realize that the Divine, out of love for us, sends us the guru to help us. God, through the guru, steps down His consciousness to the level where we can actually relate to and commune with Him.

Does everybody need a guru? That depends on what you're looking for. The plain fact is that there aren't very many people who are worthy to have a guru. You don't have a guru merely by coming onto the spiritual path. It isn't that easy. You've got to win the right to have a guru, just as you've got to win the right to study with a great artist. He's not going to waste his time with kindergarten children because he knows it's a waste of energy.

Toward the end of his life Yogananda said, "I'm tired of dealing with old nags. I want race horses now." On another occasion he said, "If you try to awaken some people when they're asleep, they'll just roll over and say, 'Let me sleep.' Others will wake up for a time, but if you leave them alone, they'll go to sleep again. Then there are some who if you just call their names, they're up, ready to go, and just keep going." That's the kind of disciple who is really fit for the kind of discipline that a guru can give. It's not a question of the guru wanting followers, or that some people are specially chosen. It's a matter of being of a high enough caliber to be able to receive what the guru has to give.

In his book, *The Holy Science,* Sri Yukteswar explains that the first thing one needs to develop in order to be able to draw the blessings of a real guru is the natural love of the heart. He said it's not possible to place one foot in front of the other on the spiritual path without this natural love of the heart being unfolded. It's only when that love does unfold that you become fit to follow one who is able to guide you on the pathway to the Infinite.

When we develop this natural love, we reach the point where we are fit to keep the company of a God-realized guru. At that time, is it necessary to have a guru? Well, is it necessary to have somebody who really can help you to paint well? Probably. But painting, at least, is something you can see physically and work on if you have a little native talent. It's a lot more difficult when we come to the level of spiritual training which is so subtle that we can't often see the changes we're working on. Spiritual changes are usually so slow that you can't see whether you're going in the right direction until several years have passed. The years do pass, and they implant themselves on our features and on our consciousness. It may be after many years that you suddenly wake up and say, "Oh, I was wrong in this way." How often have I heard that story! It's so much wiser to have somebody who has been on the path, who's followed it to the end, and who can tell you the right way to go.

Is it still *necessary* to have a guru? It is not necessary only if you have come into this incarnation so advanced that you are already your own guru. Remember the purpose of the guru is to make you your own guru. He's only there to help and guide you to the point where you can take over on your own. He isn't there to continue to keep you as a disciple. He's there to make you as great or even greater than he. There is no jealousy in God. A guru is trying to make you strong enough, wise enough, to be able to tread a straight path yourself, without any further help on his part.

Sometimes a disciple advances beyond the guru, but still he has that reverence for the guru, knowing that this was the channel through which God came to him. So it is that even those souls like Yogananda who are born already enlightened still play out the guru-disciple relationship to show the right example for other people. But other than such rare cases, I can only say this: No, you don't need a guru if you don't want God. But if you really want God and you want to work at it, then you do need a guru.

How to Find a Guru

How do you find a guru? I heard a true story about a man who went up into the mountains to meditate. One day, after many years of deep meditation, he was out for a walk. When he came back to his cottage he found a man sitting in the lotus pose. The man said to him, "I have come to help you." They say that when the disciple is ready, the guru appears. So we find the guru by developing our own love and by seeking God whole-heartedly. But we must remember that God is the guru—no human being can be a guru. God is the guru, and he acts through the agency of an enlightened soul. But a true guru will never take the credit to himself for being a guru.

Yogananda never accepted that he was the guru. He always said, "God is the guru." Once at a luncheon at Hollywood Church after the service, someone said to him, "I understand Dr. Lewis was your first disciple in America." Yogananda replied a little sternly, "That's what they say." She was surprised at that response. Then he explained, "I never call them *my* disciples. They're disciples of God." The true guru will always give the credit where it really belongs—to God. In fact, he has no self to take credit for. He's only conscious of being an instrument for God.

So if you want to find the guru, and have a true relationship with him, remember it should be a relationship first in God. Don't expect the intense personal relationship that people tend to get into with other human beings. A guru won't accept that.

The Guru Works Through Magnetism

The influence of the guru is like that of a magnet. When you have a bar of steel that hasn't been magnetized, its molecules are turned randomly, cancelling each other out. When you place that bar of steel next to a magnet, the influence of the magnet gradually aligns all those molecules in a north-south direction. Thus, the unmagnetized bar of steel develops its own magnetism. It doesn't take magnetism from the original magnet, it merely is influenced to align its own molecules.

We have in our subconsciousness all kinds of desires and tendencies from many, many incarnations. These desires are lodged, like molecules, as vortices of energy in the spine. When we think of all the billions of desires that we may have, we have to consider, "How can we ever fulfill all of them?" It's like trying to turn every little one of those billions of molecules in a bar of steel to a north-south direction, one by one. You turn a few, and by the time you've gotten up to the next group, the first ones are starting to turn their own way again.

Like a magnet, the guru is trying to align the vortices of energy in our spine. He's not trying to impose his consciousness on you, he's trying to help you develop your own inner powers so you can transmute all those energies toward the brain, all in a north-south direction. It isn't only he who does it; you have to do if for yourself. Those who think, "I'm a disciple of a guru now. He'll do it all for me," are mistaken. In every ashram you'll find that those disciples who really get somewhere are those who do the work themselves. They take the guidance from the guru to know what to do, but they do the work themselves. The guru helps us by giving us extra strength, by reaching down and pulling us up, but still we have to do the hard job of climbing that mountain to reach the heights.

It would help your meditations to feel that your guru is sitting inside your body, that he is doing the practices through you. Mentally ask your guru, "How should I be doing this? Show me." If you ask questions inwardly with attunement, you'll find that the answers will be forthcoming.

The way to relate to the guru is always inwardly, not outwardly. It's always by going into your spine and trying to bring the energy up. That's what makes Kriya Yoga such a wonderful science. It helps us to interiorize and raise the energy in the spine, and to magnetize the spine. What happens in this case is really quite literal. It's a literal fact that each little desire or tendency we've ever had has formed a little vortex. All that energy within you is committed to many other things.

The guru's influence is that power within us that will help to release and lift the energy within. We've also got to make the effort ourselves by Kriya Yoga, by devotion, by other kinds of yoga that raise the energy and direct it upward toward the spiritual eye. Until we achieve enlightenment, the energy of the ego is trapped at the medulla oblongata. A master has his being centered at the spiritual eye, and everything he does radiates outward from this point. The more we learn to bring all those energies upward in the spine and offer them to the point between the eyebrows, the more we will grow spiritually. The guru's only purpose is to help us do that.

Must the Guru Be Present Physically?

Does the guru have to be with you physically? No, he doesn't have to be, because it's an inner relationship. I have seen in ashrams those who were only relating outwardly to the guru for years, and never getting very far spiritually. But the really serious disciples were those who took it within, who didn't feel the need to be with the guru outwardly, but sought inner attunement. The guru's influence, a spiritual radiation to the disciple, is what matters.

Yogananda came into a body for only a few years, but his power is something that will live far longer. It's his divine mission to help people. That's why so many of his disciples who never had a chance to meet him in the flesh feel his presence so strongly. This is what allows someone like Yogananda to be a world savior.

It's also good to get guidance from successive lines of those who are in tune with the guru and understand that it is his power that flows through them. The guru will transmit his power through those who are in tune with him and can give his *diksha*, the physical touch of his blessing. He doesn't have to be living in his physical body because he has many other bodies to work through. But, again, the true goal is for you to become in tune with him inwardly, and to feel that guidance within your own self.

I've been speaking of Yogananda particularly, but of course he's not the only messenger that God has sent. You can recognize true saints by the signs that make them masters: the presence of compassion, calmness, wisdom, joy under all circumstances, devotion to God, selflessness—to mention but a few.

Do true masters try to draw people to themselves, or to God? If they're trying to draw people to God, then you are in the right hands. If they are trying to draw people to themselves, they'll weaken you rather than strengthen you.

A disciple once asked Yogananda, "Should I think of you or of Divine Mother?" Master said, "Think of Divine Mother." He didn't want people thinking of him as a person. He wanted them to understand always and without fail that it was Divine Mother, it was God, in other words, who was working through him and was his only authority for teaching anybody. The recognition of the guru must never be personal, but always impersonal, always grand, always vast. When thinking of a great master, whoever it might be, always think that you are seeing a window through which God is manifesting.

Recognizing Your Own Path

How can you recognize your own guru?—by the divine power that keeps growing within you. It isn't always easy to know. But if you follow one true path, as you grow spiritually, the time will come when you will know. Either you'll know that this is the right one, or you'll be led to the right one. There is no jealousy in the masters. They are only here to guide us along the path toward our own enlightenment. Many times Master himself would tell somebody that he wasn't their guru and would send them to someone else.

We have a divine potential within us—we are the perfect soul. So it is part of the Divine Law not only to feed this human being with little inspirations, but also to show us that which we can become. That is the goal of the guru. The guru is that human being who has attained Infinite consciousness and is able to express in his own total being, his own expanded awareness, all those things that are so far above what we know in our egoic human state.

The guru's goal is not merely to stand there like a light-house and show us what he has become. It is to send down a ray of the divine energy to our human level to lift us up, to perfect us. There may be other saints who have attained perfection, but we need only to go deep in one relationship. The deepest relationship possible for man is the one with that messenger that God has sent to the disciple. It is through this relationship with one saint, one master, that we are able to go much deeper than we can through the general blessings of many different saints.

When God sees the devotee striving, first of all he sends him different things that might help him: books, teachings, and so on. When the devotee really becomes sincere, then God draws him to a true guru. It isn't enough to be with him physi-cally—there has to be a deep spiritual bond formed inwardly. The guru's mission is (you might say he hasn't any choice in the matter because God sends him for this purpose) the sal-vation of the particular souls sent to him. For us there is no greater blessing possible in this realm of delusion.

Questions & Answers
with Swami Kriyananda

Question: Is it necessary to have a guru to advance spiritually? I don't really feel the need for one, and I have difficulty with the thought of devotion to a guru.

Kriyananda: You need a guru if you want to find God. Understand what the guru really is, for it is definitely a law of the spiritual path that to find God — indeed, to get very far at all on the spiritual path — one needs a guru. A true guru is not a man or woman, merely, but an egoless channel for the Divine. His human body and personality are the most superficial things about him. To see him as he really is is to see a blazing light shining through the narrow "window" of his humanity. You say you have difficulty with the thought of devotion to a guru, but devotion to the guru *as a man or woman* is not really what is asked of the devotee. (Though if one is thirsty, I should think a cup of water would not be scorned with the excuse that one is looking for a lake.) My guru, Paramhansa Yogananda, himself said that it is God alone who is the true Guru, acting through the agency of souls that are awake in Him.

To seek God, on the other hand, without at least *wanting* Him would be self-contradictory. To want Him is to feel devotion to Him. To feel devotion to Him is to love Him in all His manifestations, ignorant as well as wise. Inevitably, then, the true devotee feels special love for those great souls who manifest Him most purely.

What one should look to is God's impersonal presence manifested in the guru, and not merely to the guru himself as a human being. Master himself taught us this kind of devotion and always discouraged too personal an affection for him.

———

Question: What is the difference between a spiritual teacher and a guru? Many people are willing to accept a teacher, but the guru concept as an embodiment of God, as a perfect being, is a problem for them.

Kriyananda: I would say that they are quite different. There are a lot of gurus around that are not true gurus. To be a true guru, a person has to be already united with God. He has to know the consciousness of the Infinite. It's like the difference between going to St. Francis of Assisi for instruction in the spiritual life, and going to a novice leader who hasn't any kind of realization himself. Jesus called it, "The blind leading the blind." They will both fall into a ditch. That doesn't mean that spiritual teachers are bad, but they have to recognize their limitations. They have to see that they don't have all the answers. They have to be honest about what they really are and aren't, at least to the extent that they are capable of seeing themselves.

A teacher is one who has some experience, who is capable of guiding you to a certain point, and is perhaps capable of transmitting some spiritual power, but he would not be a guru. Therefore people who want to go higher need to be guided by a soul who has achieved full realization.

———

Chapter 2

THE DISCIPLE'S PART

Words of Paramhansa Yogananda

When I met my guru, Swami Sri Yukteswar, he said to me, "Allow me to discipline you."

"Why sir?" I inquired.

"When I encountered my guru, Lahiri Mahasaya," he replied, "my will was guided by whims. But when I attuned my will to Lahiri Mahasaya's wisdom-guided will, my own will became free, because guided by wisdom."

In the same way, I discovered that by attuning my will to Sri Yukteswar's wisdom-guided will, my will, too, became free.

This is the purpose of discipleship, and of the obedience that it entails. The aim of obedience to the guru is not to enslave the disciple, but to liberate his will from that which enslaves it truly: whims, and much more—bondage to likes and dislikes, and to desires and attachments.

Most people consider it an affirmation of freedom to indulge their desires "freely." They don't see that desire itself is compulsive. It blinds their discrimination. Where is the freedom in any act that leads one more deeply into delusion? Spiritual healing requires willing cooperation on the disciple's part. It cannot be achieved by passivity. Surrender to the divine will, as expressed through the guru, must be offered freely, willingly, and intelligently.

—*The Essence of Self-Realization: The Wisdom of Paramhansa Yogananda*, by Swami Kriyananda. *See Resources.*

The Disciple's Part
Taken from Talks by Swami Kriyananda

The guru-disciple relationship is perhaps the most important relationship the soul can have in this world of relativity. It is also the most important relationship the ego can have in the sense that it's the one relationship that thoroughly demolishes the ego. The worldly person, however, doesn't see the attractiveness of this relationship; he doesn't like to put himself in the position of subordination to what he considers to be just another person. He feels that his opinion is as good as anyone else's. In the matter of seeking God, he doesn't see the need for another human being to intercede, but thinks to establish his own relationship with God directly.

It's very important to speak not only of why we need a guru, but more particularly of how we can be good disciples. This is an even more difficult question, and one that, generally speaking, people don't understand on a deep level.

A true disciple is not somebody who is always trying to proselytize others, or who goes around outwardly saying, "Oh, Master, Master, Master." Neither is he somebody who acts as though he were a member of a special club. A true disciple, first of all, has to have the right attitudes that make him a good disciple. Increasingly he has to develop that kind of consciousness which the guru brings to him.

Discipleship to the Infinite

In the beginning it's absolutely inescapable that the disciple will see the guru only in human terms. After all, the guru has a body, a personality, an ego—all the things necessary to make a body function. But the guru resides in his own Self and watches these things. As Master wrote in his beautiful poem, *Samadhi,* "I, the cosmic sea, watch the little ego floating in me." There has to be an ego, or the body couldn't be sustained, but it's a different kind of ego. It's not the ego of pride or of identification with an individual consciousness. In a sense you could say there is no ego, because the deeper meaning of ego is the soul identified with the body. A great master is not identified with the body at all. He merely sits back, watches, and directs it.

There was a period of time when I was out at Master's desert retreat with him. Every evening after finishing that day's dictation on his commentaries on the *Bhagavad Gita,* he used to go out for a walk with me. He would walk quite slowly because he was in a very deep state of consciousness. At this time he was manifesting the wisdom aspect of God, and was very impersonal. Sometimes he would rest his hand on my forearm for support as we walked along. Then he would stop, sway back and forth, and lean on me so he wouldn't fall over. Once he said, "It's so difficult to know which body I'm supposed to keep moving when I feel myself equally present in all bodies."

It took great effort on his part just to hold his mind down to that little body. You might even say that it's as difficult for a master to keep his mind down on our level as it is for us to get up to his, except he can make it and we can't. But we must remember that we can. We must not constantly think of our limited humanity, but always inwardly think of our divinity. This is one of the attitudes that is so necessary for a true disciple.

The Need for Right Attitude

First of all, we need to develop attitudes of humility, of wanting to learn, of being willing to give up one's own desires, of giving up one's normal human tendency to justify oneself, to insist on being right. Unfortunately it's all too common for disciples to act as if the guru were some sort of heavenly slave, always doing them little favors. You find this sort of person saying, "Oh, Master did this for me, or, Master did that for me." They don't understand what Master is. They reduce Master to the level of a human personality, when he is so much more.

I heard a story about a disciple of Master which was sweet in a way, but didn't seem to me to express right understanding. This disciple was on a plane that began to have engine trouble and was forced to circle the airport several times. Fearing for the lives of all those on board, the disciple began to pray. Then he decided that he'd better not pray to Master because he had such a sense of humor he'd probably make them circle one more time before letting them come down. So he prayed to Babaji. Well, that is a cute story, but it doesn't satisfy me.

Master did have a wonderful sense of humor, but people often treat him as though that was all he was: a wonderful person, a wonderful smile, a lovely sense of humor, a great love for people, and so on. He was all of that, but he was something so much more. Even in the midst of laughing with you, he had such depth in his eyes that it was like melting into an ocean to look into them. To say he was this, or that he was anything, is to sell him short. He was everything. He was so above it all that the only way to really be a true disciple was to try to *be* that, too. There was no separation between him and us, but it was much more than that—he was in our hearts already. He knew everything we thought. He knows everything you think right now. He showed this to us again and again. How one man could know every single thought of every one of his disciples was always beyond imagination to me, but he proved it to us again and again. He said, "I know every single thought every one of you is thinking." How are you to be a true disciple of someone like that?

Letting Go of the Ego

The first step in becoming a true disciple is to be a proper human being—that means relinquishing those things that prevent one from attaining the state of consciousness of the guru. What is a human being in its improper human state? First of all, it clings to that state. It says, "I am real. My body is real; my personality is real; my ego is real." Secondly, it says, "I am more real than anyone else. If they suffer, I don't feel it. If I suffer, however, I do feel it. Therefore I am more real. When I am happy, I feel it. When other people are happy, I'm happy for them, but in a different way!"

It is that the ego is willing to set itself in opposition to other people. It's willing to take things from others, and to do things that may hurt them, so long as it helps itself. This kind of person gets into the competition, warfare, struggle, and suffering that is part of the ego-centered consciousness. He upholds his own desires and their fulfillment at all costs. He doesn't want to set himself into submission, into discipleship to another human being. After all, this is diminishing the very thing that is most precious to him—the sense of separate identity.

To be a true disciple, we need also to have the attitude of openness to the guru, to be willing to be corrected at any time. We have to be disciples as much at the end of the path as we were at the beginning. Once Master said to Rajarshi (his most advanced disciple), who had already attained *nirbikalpa samadhi,* "Don't forget where your power comes from." Though he was a multimillionaire, as well as a highly advanced yogi, Rajarshi said, just like a little boy, "I won't Master. It comes from you."

The love that you find between the master and the disciple, when the disciple has gotten out of his ego and there is only God sharing with God, is so sweet and beautiful. We would see Master and Rajarshi walking around the grounds hand in hand and just gazing at everything with such wonder because they were seeing God there.

To be a true disciple, we must be open to life, open to truth wherever we find it. In that way, we find many opportunities for growth. In that openness which is true humility, we find that we can learn from the stones, from the clouds, from everything.

Tests for the Disciple

The way of the disciple is not easy. The guru asks things of us that are not convenient, and the ego goes through certain tests because of this. Every devotee on the path goes through the same basic tests, though each one will have his own individual challenges as well. The first is negativity. Invariably it happens when you first come onto the path that someone tries to turn you away from it. Someone will say negative things, and you start to listen. Either you are swayed towards this negativity, or you resist and say no.

Once Master's own father was starting to say certain things against Sri Yukteswar. Master cut him off, saying, "Of all things! Human birth is something, but divine birth is everything. If you ever say one more word against my guru, I will disown you as my father." From then on his father never said a thing against Sri Yukteswar. Everybody goes through this test in one way or another. It's just part of the path. It's part of delusion's effort to pull you back.

You can tell if something is the pull of delusion or not by the kind of consciousness you develop from it. Does it give you peace? Does it give you joy? Or does it undermine that peace and joy? Those things that are from God help to develop more divine states of consciousness. Those that are born of delusion take away that attunement and destroy it. People who follow the negative path don't become more peaceful or more in tune, but lose their attunement and fall back into egotism and selfishness.

The next test that comes along is a certain rebelliousness. The disciple thinks, "You are asking too much of me. I am not going to do that much. I've got my life to lead, too." The disciple doesn't want to be asked to give up everything because that doesn't seem fair. So, in reaction, he rebels.

The third test is the thought, "What the guru is saying may be right for him and for a few others, but he doesn't understand me and my needs." Sister Gyanamata, Yogananda's most advanced woman disciple, was a very old woman, quite frail and ill, when she moved to Mt. Washington. So great was her dedication that, though her body was very sick, she would unceasingly run up and down the stairs serving her guru. It didn't matter to her because she never thought about herself.

A couple of disciples said to her, "You've got your own will, too. You shouldn't just make yourself a slave to his will." She replied, "Well, I'm a little too old now to change. Furthermore, I have never known such happiness in my life as I do now being in tune with my Guru."

Tuning In To the Guru's Will

It's inevitable that you will get some of these tests, but the way out of them is to be a good disciple. This means always trying to attune to the guru's will, always trying to do what the guru wants. The guru's will is expressed in various ways. Even while Master was with us in the body, his will was expressed more inwardly than outwardly. Very often he would express himself outwardly in a way that would completely confound reason. An example of this was when he gave me the job of editing his *Bhagavad Gita* interpretations. My assigned task was to "edit" the magazine articles that appeared in the 30's and 40's. He said, "Work like lightning; there's no time to be lost. But, don't change a word." How I was to edit and not change a word, I never did figure out. He would throw you such curves that sometimes you just didn't know what he was talking about. The reason was that he wanted you to go inside and understand inwardly what he wanted. I don't mean that he never gave specific outward advice and instructions. Of course he did, but more than that he wanted you to understand with your consciousness.

There was one disciple that Master was scolding about something, and the disciple said, "Yes, Master, I know. I understand what you are saying." Master said, "You don't understand. If you understood, you'd *do* what I'm saying."

The fact is that knowing the words and understanding the concepts aren't enough. Master was trying to get his consciousness into our consciousness so that we would really understand him, and then act. Until we are able to act in attunement, until that real understanding is reached, we are not obeying even when we go through the outward motions, because it's a superficial thing.

Loyalty–The First Law of God

The most important aspect of being a true disciple and overcoming the tests on the path is the commitment of loyalty—the commitment of trust. Master said that loyalty is the first law of God. Even while he was living, many disciples would go rushing from one teacher to another, but they didn't get God. One has to be loyal to one's way, to the way God has sent. By doing this, loyalty becomes such a direct pipeline to the spirit that we're totally absorbed in that vibration. Many disciples will think, "I'll take so much of the guru's teachings, but no more." We have to make as our very first premise an acceptance of what he said.

This has always been my guideline since I first came onto the path. I was so new, I didn't know anything. A week before I came to Master, I had never even heard the words "guru," or "yoga," or "karma," or any of the things we take so much for granted now. When I came I was in a state of mental turmoil with all the new thoughts being thrown at me right and left by disciples who took them for granted.

The only way out for me was to have absolute faith in Master's integrity. Sometimes what the other disciples said didn't make any sense, but I would ask, "Did Master say it?"

If the answer was yes, then I'd accept it. If it wasn't, then I'd battle it out. We must have this as our starting point, if we're going to be good disciples.

There may be things that other teachers say that seem contradictory. This is part of the realm of relativity—that you cannot say anything without excluding some things that are perhaps equally as true. So it is necessary to follow one guru. They are all saying basically the same thing, but they put it in different ways, which to our limited understanding doesn't seem the same. Again this is why it is necessary to follow only one way. Otherwise you have your feet in two boats, and you fall in the middle and drown. I've seen this happen to devotees if they read too much of different spiritual teachings. There are certain things that different great ones said that, to the beginner's understanding, seem conflicting.

I remember a beautiful thing that a great saint in India once said to me. I had questioned him about something he had said that seemed to contradict Master. He said, "If all the disciples of masters really understood their masters, there wouldn't be all the quarreling that you find in religion." In other words, he wasn't really saying something different from Master. It merely looked that way to me because I hadn't yet understood on a deep enough level. Until there is that level of understanding, commit yourself to one way.

Discipleship Means Giving Everything to God

As well as tests, every devotee goes through ups and downs on the path. During his ups there are times when he feels as if God were practically a hair's breadth away. He only has a bit further to go, and he'll be there. Everyone goes through such periods where he feels so in tune that he's really, as it were, just racing towards heaven. Then all of a sudden that quality is lost, and the clouds roll in again, and he wonders what ever happened.

We can understand it this way: as soon as we get a divine state of consciousness, the strength of delusion is such that we take the blessing to ourselves, and think that we're special or important. We get a little experience of God, and instead of expressing appreciation, we start to think, "Oh, I've got something now. I'm someone special now." The ego comes in again, and because of this we come crashing down and have to begin all over again.

The way out is for all our energies to always be directed towards God. The true disciple is always thinking only of how he can serve God and guru more, of what more he can give. If the devotee starts to think of how he can get more experience or more realization, then he falls back into delusion. It has to be a constant giving, and in that giving, God can give us more. It's like a closed circuit that builds up greater and greater power.

We have to become empty vessels, to drain ourselves of that which is human in order that the Divine might fill us. So it is that we must get away from thinking of our relationship with the guru in a purely human way. The guru is omnipresent. As true disciples, we should try to become omnipresent like him.

A true disciple should not be thinking of just himself and the guru, or of the guru as a human being who resides in time and space. We should think of ourselves in a more impersonal way. We should try always to develop those inner qualities to such an impersonal degree that our love is no longer the love of a human being for another human being. It's the love of the Infinite for the Infinite, of the Unknown for the Unknown, or as one great saint said, "Of the Alone for the Alone." We are always alone in this universe. There is nothing, in the last analysis, but you and God. Everything else is only a way-station along the way. As Master used to say often, "I killed Yogananda long ago. No one dwells in this temple now but God."

We are not just humble little devotees stumbling along making mistakes. We are that Infinite Light. We are that Infinite Wisdom. We are that Divine Soul. Master's mission was to show us that we are that. Until we achieve that realization, we will not have fulfilled to perfection this most wonderful of all relationships—the relationship of the guru and the disciple.

Questions & Answers
with Swami Kriyananda

Question: What was your greatest test when you first came onto the path?

Kriyananda: I was a doubter at heart. In fact, that was probably my greatest flaw on the path—the tendency to think there had to be something wrong, to look for the flaw, to find the fly in the ointment. But from the first moment that I began reading *Autobiography of a Yogi*, I was convinced that Yogananda was a great being and the only person I'd ever come in contact with in my life that I could completely trust. I accepted this on an intuitive level, but my mind had the habit of challenging, questioning, doubting, and so on.

I think probably the greatest period of testing that I went through was questioning and doubting Master's wisdom, not so much on a spiritual level but on a human level. I know this sounds ridiculous, but then I was being ridiculous, I suppose. It's something I had to work out. Master would say that something meant a certain thing, but on the other hand it could also mean something else. It took me a long time to come to appreciate how much more sophisticated that way of thinking was because truth is like a many-faceted diamond.

In time I came to understand that he was just looking at truth from different angles to give us a much bigger picture. In retrospect, this doubting seems absurd, but it was a real test for me at that time. I eventually found that the answer to this dilemma was not to be realized on an intellectual level. It was solvable only on a heart level. As I came to love him more deeply my doubting dissolved, and with its dissolution suddenly a deeper intellectual understanding came as well.

Question: You've mentioned practicing the presence of God. What if a person doesn't have a guru? Brother Lawrence wrote about talking to God as if He were right there with you.

Kriyananda: Whatever other technique you do, this is something you should do all the time—practice the presence of God. Words are not the important thing. The important thing is that you have your mind always centered within and watching everything that you're doing as if it weren't really yours. With or without yoga techniques, you'll never get anywhere if you don't have that attitude.

I would say the important thing is not to go looking for a guru. Look for God. God will send you what you need at the time that you need it. Our devotion should always be to God. I remember Yogananda saying to one disciple, "Never mind what happens to me. Don't forget God." God is our common Father. He's the one we're looking for.

Chapter 3

ATTUNEMENT
WITH THE GURU

Words of Paramhansa Yogananda

Attunement to the guru means complete, heartfelt acceptance of his guidance, and also of his activities. Your acceptance must be unqualified. You mustn't say, for instance, "I accept what the guru tells me in this situation, but not in that one." Nor should you say, "I accept what he tells me, but not what those tell me whom he has appointed to represent him."

Attunement means also listening for the guru's inner guidance, in your heart. In everything, ask him mentally what you should do; how you should behave; how you can love God more deeply. More than guidance, ask him to give you the power to develop spiritually.

Be guided by common sense also. Never, in the name of attunement, behave in such a way as to offend against reason or against the rules of proper conduct. "Learn to behave," Sri Yukteswar used to say. Don't let attunement with the guru, in other words, be your excuse for an undisciplined imagination!

To tune in to the guru's consciousness, visualize him in the spiritual eye. Mentally call to him there. Imagine his eyes, gazing at you. Invite his consciousness to inspire your own.

Then, after calling to him for some time, try to feel his response in your heart. The heart is the center of intuition in the body. It is your "radio-receiver."

Your "broadcasting station" is situated in the Christ-Consciousness center between the eyebrows. It is from this center that your will broadcasts into the universe your thoughts and ideas.

Once you feel an answer in the heart, call to the guru deeply, "Introduce me to God."

—*The Essence of Self-Realization: The Wisdom of Paramhansa Yogananda*, by Swami Kriyananda. *See Resources.*

Attunement with the Guru
Taken from Talks by Swami Kriyananda

In the Indian language, the word "disciple" has quite a different meaning than it does in English, one that implies a much sweeter and more personal relationship. In the West, we think of a disciple as somebody who is willing to accept discipline and be molded by the teacher—which is perfectly valid, and very much a part of what discipleship to a great master means. There is, however, another connotation that is left out when we think only in terms of discipline.

In India, the difference between *siksha,* or student, and *chela,* or disciple, is the difference between somebody who is out there taking notes but not really committed, and somebody who is your child. The *chela* is, in fact, thought of as the child of the guru. This includes being disciplined and taught, but more importantly, it means having a close, loving relationship with the guru, being a part of his family, and an heir to his spiritual wealth.

I'm reminded of a time at the Lake Shrine when Master was putting on musical programs for the public. Visitors would see the lovely surroundings, listen to a beautiful concert under the stars, and then they would go away. Referring to them, Master once said, "Those who are *not* our own come, enjoy themselves for awhile, and then they go. But those who *are* our own never leave." This is, in fact, quite true. Those true disciples who leave outwardly are never really gone. They are never able to get Master out of their hearts because this connection is put there by God.

This loving soul-contact is the essence of what Master came to bring into our lives. You can get spiritual teachings from books, but what the great masters really bring is their consciousness. What we must try to do as disciples is tune in with Master's consciousness, his loving presence and guidance, in every act of our lives.

It's not enough to read books on how others have done it, or to push aside our inner contact with him while we try to be practical. Of course, we have to be practical, too, but we must develop that kind of faith, that kind of discipleship, that draws on the inner guidance of Master to answer all the questions in our lives.

What has made the religions of India so vital down through thousands of years? They don't have an organized church—you might say it's the most disorganized religion in the world. Yet the Indian culture has an innate respect for living expressions of the spiritual teachings, for the guru. They lovingly draw upon these expressions, so the Divine keeps coming into manifestation there again and again. With all the folly, superficiality, and errors that creep into religion, this single truth has kept religion alive in India throughout the ages—that through personal attunement with those who know God, others can find realization themselves.

What is the most important thing we can do as disciples? Be in tune, and when things get difficult, get more in tune. The greatest thing that Master has to give us is that attunement. His teaching, his mission—all of these things are very important, yes—but secondary to that attunement.

Silence is the Altar of God

Remember there have been great masters who never spoke a word, and yet were able to bring their disciples to God. When Master was with guests, he was the most charming host you could imagine. He would have lunch with them, share beautiful truths, and regale them with jokes or lovely stories. Often guests would say to the monks and nuns who lived in the ashram, "How lucky you are to be with that kind of energy all the time! What a blessing you have!" We would gently smile, because the fact was that he would encourage the disciples to keep silence around him.

Master often told us, "Silence is the altar of God." He said only in silence can you really feel God's presence. When you allow the mind to become restless with thoughts and desires, then you bring yourself down to a level where God can't communicate with you.

God's body is space. If you want to feel him, you must feel space in your body and all around it. The same is true with silence. God's voice is silence. If you really want to commune with Him, it must be done in the silence of your own mind, and then in the silence of the Infinite. In that silence you will hear the voice of the Infinite booming with the great power of AUM all through creation. First, we must try to empty our consciousness of ego, and then to re-fill it in a divine way.

As disciples of this great master, we are naturally moved by the things he said and did. We are naturally caught up in his personality, because that's what we can see, but we must always remember that he was so much more. It used to be difficult for me when I would meditate on Master's presence within, and then he would come into the room. I would be feeling him inside, and then would think, "What's he doing out there?" It's hard to shake that delusion.

In this respect, it's a lot easier for those who never saw him to feel him solely within. Living with him, however, was sometimes confusing for me, because at the same time that I was trying to feel him inside, I could hear him talking in the next room. Once he even teased me when I was trying to feel him in this way—he came up to me, looked me straight in the eyes, and handed me an apple!

Tuning into Omnipresence

A great master lives in omnipresence, and his teaching is from that level of reality. He doesn't spell out in exact detail the whole truth that he's trying to convey. Each of us as disciples has to go deep into that truth, understand its essence, and from attunement with it, manifest that ray in our life.

Did Master say anything about how an accountant should conduct himself when filling up a ledger? I don't think so. Does this mean that therefore an accountant cannot use Master's teachings while filling up a ledger? Of course, he can.

You see, we have to apply that truth. We have to go deeply into whatever Master said. When I started Ananda I had very few guidelines, especially for all the things that have come up ever since. Many of these things have needed instant decisions, and I couldn't go rushing off to books to read what Master said before I came back with an answer. I've had to tune in with him. You, too, must tune in with him as a master to realize that his reality is in you—not a reality that was born in 1893, or that died in 1952.

Master opened a particular doorway in the vast ocean of consciousness, and said, "If you come in here, you'll be able to go deep." What you need to do is meditate deeply on his words—on even one phrase that he uttered, choosing things that have special meaning for you. Go behind the teachings, and in silence try to perceive their heartbeat, their essence. Then try to use that essence creatively in your daily life. If you do this and spiritualize that truth, it will change your life.

What Master came to bring us was, indeed, a specific message and mission. We are fulfilling a part of that mission at Ananda. We've done it with his grace—and only with his grace has it been possible. That grace is a power you can tune in to, if you will, just like electricity. You plug into the electric current from the city, and then you have the power to light an electric light. So tune into Master's presence, and ask him to guide you. Be in tune—that's what he used to say to us.

The Real Attunement

It's one thing to read Yogananda's books, yet it was another thing to have lived with him, and to have seen his example. In *Autobiography of a Yogi,* you read about many miracles. Indeed, many things of a miraculous nature happened around him, but he never talked about them. He talked only about devotion.

When you think of his teachings, one imagines that he would sit there and give us all sorts of instructions. He put me in charge of organizing the monks, and you'd think that he would have had long talks with me on what he wanted. Several times, in fact, he said that he wanted to talk about it, but he never did! What he really wanted me to do—what he wants us all to do—is to tune into his consciousness.

In *Autobiography of a Yogi,* Master says that Lahiri Mahasaya's interpretations of the *Bhagavad Gita* were often done by Lahiri's disciples tuning into him, and then writing the words. It was Lahiri Mahasaya who inspired them to write what they did, and it was completely in tune with his teaching. This is discipleship; this is real attunement.

All the time when Master was with us, he would say, "Be in tune, be in tune." He talked about it as the most important thing he could give to us, because through that attunement he is always able to inspire us with the right decisions, the right understanding, in every situation.

Developing Our Own Intuition

I've seen it happen so often that through intuition born of attunement, an answer to a question I had been seeking, sometimes even for years, will suddenly come. It's important to try to develop our intuition, but it's also easy to be fooled. I don't want to kid myself, and much less you, with the thought of something being intuition when it isn't. It's very hard to know. Therefore, I always say tentatively, "Well, it seems so." That seeming, however, is usually born of a real feeling inside—I never presume.

Over many years, I have found that feeling born out objectively, because when that particular intuitive sense is there, things seem to work out well. We shouldn't depend on someone else's attunement or intuition, however. Master came to teach us that this is something we all have to develop.

Very often Master's reply to a very deep or important question would be only a hint—something for you to work on so that you could develop your own inner wisdom. What he passed on was not a body of specific things to be learned by rote; it was an attunement with a ray of divine light.

As you tune in to that ray, you will make mistakes—I certainly have made my share. You don't want to bring yourself to the point where you think, "I'm always right." As soon as you have that thought, Divine Mother will say, "Aha, time for a lesson!" You must have the humility before God to know that you could be mistaken. Your personality, your desires, your attachments, your likes and dislikes, your way of thinking as opposed to somebody else's way—are all too likely to prejudice a flow which in itself is completely universal and impersonal. Truth can be just as much on the side of a drunk as on the side of a saint.

So we must move forward with tentativeness and humility—and yet, with faith. That's why Master used to say the spiritual path is like walking a tightrope. How can you be tentative, and yet have faith? Offer everything to God and guru, and use your common sense because real faith has to be kept in a state of reason or it becomes dogmatic.

Therefore, with that degree of tentative self-offering, rely more and more on the guidance that you feel from within. You will find that in little ways, and then in big ways, you will be guided. This loving guidance will be with you in amazing ways, and constantly.

Finding the Divine Solution

I often went to Master with questions, but then I would discover, after I had left his presence, that I had not asked one of them. I'd feel frustrated with myself, until I realized that I didn't ask the questions because he'd given me the answers.

In other words, the answers to our questions often are not intellectual, verbal formulae. Our real question is, "How do I get peace? How do I get that state of consciousness where I have understanding on my own?" In his presence we had that, and we saw there was nothing to question.

Questions come when your mind is on a lower level of functioning. You don't have anything to question when you are in superconsciousness. As Ramakrishna used to say, "The bumblebee makes a lot of noise before it enters the flower. Once inside, it's silent because it's sucking nectar."

In his daily example, Master taught us how being in that state of attunement answered everything. We should make every effort to tune in more deeply with that guidance from Master. He's the real power in whatever we try to do. He brought from God a ray of the Infinite which we can tune into. As Lahiri Mahasaya said to Master's mother, "Your son will be a mighty locomotive that will draw many, many souls to God's kingdom." Master said many would find God through him after his passing.

If you tune in to the ray of divine light, you will recognize that Master was not a man who came to America, built an organization, wrote books, and had great depth and a wonderful sense of humor. He wasn't any of that. He was the power of God.

Once a disciple wrote him a note, saying, "When I see you, I only see Divine Mother there." Master didn't giggle and blush, or make self-deprecating remarks. What he did do was tap the disciple lightly with his cane, and say, "Then behave accordingly." That's what he is—a window for Divine Mother to talk to us, to bring us what we need.

As it says in the Bible, "As many as received him, to them gave He the power to become the sons of God." That power is in Master, as in Christ, and He can give it to you, but only if you tune in. How can you tune in? By always keeping his presence in your heart, by always referring your thoughts, your needs, your questions, your quest for guidance back to that inner presence.

"To those who think me near," Master said, "I will be near." Think him with you now, because He is with you. He has that power to make you—his child—one with God.

Questions & Answers
with Swami Kriyananda

Question: Why do some teachers claim that you must have a living guru, when Paramhansa Yogananda said he would continue to be the guru of people who were drawn to his teachings after he left this world?

Kriyananda: The question you raise is one which many people have asked me. I certainly do not think that Master would have told people that he would continue to be the guru and to bring people to God after his *mahasamadhi* if he hadn't meant it. Moreover, considering that he was truly an enlightened master, I don't believe he could have said and meant it without also knowing what he was talking about.

But this is the dogmatic approach to your question. We must also think things through for ourselves, or we'll end up merely parroting the wise sayings of others, without ever becoming wise. Here, then, is how I view the matter in its various ramifications.

There are many channels for Master's help and grace. First and foremost, there is our own contact with him in meditation. Second, there is the channel of disciples who are in tune with him. Third, there is the channel of innumerable people and experiences in our lives, through which he instructs and disciplines us from time to time. Master himself told me an interesting and, I think, little-known point of spiritual law. He said that there must be at least one physical contact between the guru and the disciple at some point on the spiritual path. But even while he was physically living he didn't make this contact with every disciple personally. Sometimes he asked me or one of the other disciples to initiate individuals on his own behalf. If the necessary physical contact could be made through the channel of disciples while he was still living physically, it becomes clear how he fulfills his promise to be the guru to newcomers after his *mahasamadhi*. The contact can still be made through disciples who themselves received the grace of his physical touch, and in whom, through their continued attunement with him, he is still very much alive. Thus we may also see the principal way in which the contact with a great master can be perpetuated through successive "generations" of disciples. (A master can also, of course, work through others who are highly advanced enough to receive his grace directly. He told me, for example, that Jesus appeared to the great master, Sri Ramakrishna, in the last century and asked him to liberate a certain disciple of his, once fallen, who had at last expiated his great sin.)

The criterion for the perpetuation of this physical contact with the guru is not the simple fact of formal initiation as a disciple. Initiation alone does not even constitute discipleship, really. I remember one devotee who had received Kriya Yoga initiation numerous times from Master himself, but who left the path during my early years in the monastery. Certain other disciples had been leaving during this period also. (Towards the end of a great master's life there seems usually to be a sort of spiritual "house cleaning." Disciples who are not fully dedicated feel his mental withdrawal, and imagine that he has become cold towards them. They miss his smiles and laughter, and are not developed enough inwardly to feel his continued, subtle blessing on their souls.) During this period, Master was sometimes asked how long it would take for this person or that to come back to him. "In his next incarnation," Master sometimes replied, or, "In two or three lives." But of the disciple I have just referred to, Master, when asked the same question, answered, "He will never come back. He was never in." Yet, as I said this person was initiated into formal discipleship many times by Master personally.

Obviously, then, initiation alone is not enough. Nor is any outward formality or merely institutional ordination. What counts is one's *inner* sense of attunement, his own deep, personal realization of the guru's living presence. I once asked Master, "After you are gone, will you be as much with us as you are now?" He replied, "To those who think me near, I shall be near." The disciple must be inwardly in tune. The deeper his attunement, the more perfect an instrument he becomes also for the guru's grace.

But his own attunement is not the only important factor in the transfer of that grace. The persons he initiates and blesses must be receptive also. Ultimately, remember, it is God alone who is the guru. It is God's power, through the guru, that the disciples transmit to others. The guru is a guru indeed only because of his complete openness to the flow of divine grace. It is this openness alone which determines the spiritual fitness of anyone, both to receive and to transmit.

Chapter 4

LIFE WITH A MASTER

Words of Paramhansa Yogananda

In Master's life (here Yogananda is referring to his Guru, Sri Yukteswar) I fully discovered the cleavage between spiritual realism and the obscure mysticism that spuriously passes as a counterpart. My guru was reluctant to discuss the super-physical realms. His only "marvelous" aura was one of perfect simplicity. In conversation he avoided startling references; in action he was freely expressive. Others talked of miracles but could manifest nothing; Sri Yukteswar seldom mentioned the subtle laws but secretly operated them at will.

"A man of realization does not perform any miracle until he receives an inward sanction," Master explained. "God does not wish the secrets of His creation revealed promiscuously. Also, every individual in the world has inalienable right to his free will. A saint will not encroach upon that independence."

The silence habitual to Sri Yukteswar was caused by his deep perceptions of the Infinite. No time remained for the interminable "revelations" that occupy the days of teachers without self-realization. "In shallow men the fish of little thoughts cause much commotion. In oceanic minds the whales of inspiration make hardly a ruffle." This observation from the Hindu scriptures is not without discerning humor.

Because of my guru's unspectacular guise, only a few of his contemporaries recognized him as a superman. The popular adage: "He is a fool that cannot conceal his wisdom," could never be applied to Sri Yukteswar. Though born a mortal like all others, Master had achieved identity with the Ruler of time and space. In his life I perceived a godlike unity. He had not found any insuperable obstacle to mergence of human with

Divine. No such barrier exists, I came to understand, save in man's spiritual unadventurousness.

I always thrilled at the touch of Sri Yukteswar's holy feet. Yogis teach that a disciple is spiritually magnetized by reverent contact with a master; a subtle current is generated. The devotee's undesirable habit-mechanisms in the brain are often cauterized; the groove of his worldly tendencies beneficially disturbed. Momentarily at least he may find the secret veils of *maya* lifting, and glimpse the reality of bliss. My whole body responded with a liberating glow whenever I knelt in the Indian fashion before my guru.

—*Autobiography of a Yogi,* the original 1946 unedited edition, by Paramhansa Yogananda. *See Resources.*

Life with a Master
Taken from Talks by Swami Kriyananda

How Yogananda Trained His Disciples

I first came upon *Autobiography of a Yogi* in a New York bookstore in September 1948. I bought it, read it non-stop in three days, then took the next bus to California to meet Yogananda. Of all the people I've met, and God knows I've met many tens of thousands, none has inspired me so much as Master. Before reading that book, I didn't even know what a master was, nor had I ever heard the word "guru." I had always held the opinion that I wouldn't follow anyone in my life, but only follow my own inner light. When I read that book, however, I felt that here was somebody who could help me find what I was looking for.

After meeting Master, I knew he was the one person of all I had ever met, or could even imagine meeting, that I would be willing to follow. Living with him, I came to see what spiritual greatness was, at least to the extent I was capable of understanding it at that time. Sometimes he didn't meet my expectations of greatness; sometimes I had to think through things that he would say or do. Each time I did, however, I discovered he was greater, not lesser, than my expectations.

I was shocked very soon after coming to him, because I had assumed a master was always grave and never laughed, and that everything he said was like an oracle. I had been with him for about a month when he took some of us to the desert retreat at Twenty-Nine Palms. He called me into his room one evening, brought out a little paper bag, and then he turned out the lights. I heard a crinkling sound and a little bit of chuck-ling, and then suddenly I saw sparks flying across the room. He had one of those little pistols that shoot blue sparks. Next he turned on the lights and had another pistol which shot something up in the air. It became a little parachute and floated slowly down. I was stunned. He asked me, "How do you like them?" Feeling rather embarrassed, I replied, "They're fine, sir." Then he looked at me penetratingly, and said, "Suffer little children to come unto me, for of such is the kingdom of God." I was deeply moved by this incident.

The Guru Teaches in Varying Ways

So many times Yogananda would be in a playful mood, and yet the playing itself would be a kind of lesson. The way he taught was often indirect, as though through the back door. At the time you might only suspect that he was giving you a lesson, but somehow years later you would look back and see clearly what he had in mind. He also had an enormous sense of humor and fun. It wasn't as if everything had to be some kind of cosmic lesson. He was the most unpretentious, humble person I ever met. He never thought to accept any-body's devotion to himself, but always directed it toward God.

There were so many levels to his consciousness. I've never met a master or a saint, what to speak of an ordinary human being, who was so balanced. Some saints will be great in their love, or compassion, or wisdom, but he was great in every-thing. When he was in the *bhav*, or attitude, of wisdom, he was like a Himalayan yogi in a cave. Then everything he said was a pearl of such profundity that it was thrilling. Yet a moment later he could be laughing and playing like a child.

Once some of the children were meditating when they began to feel something hitting them on the back of the head. It turned out that Master was shooting spitballs at them. He roared with laughter, yet one moment later he could be totally detached. He had absolute control over himself from one moment to the next. I even noticed that in the midst of his laughter, you could look into his eyes, and it would be like looking into an ocean, completely untouched. His laughter was just a little ripple on the surface of his mind, for he was beyond everything.

Sometimes it was a little awkward to be around him, because in a way it wasn't like being with a human being at all. I always had the feeling that God himself was present. Even when he was playing or laughing or talking about digging a ditch, one couldn't help feeling his divinity.

Omniscience of the Guru

Occasionally when he was speaking, little thoughts would run through our minds relating to what he was saying. At that moment he would look at us as if he knew exactly what we were thinking. Other times, while in the midst of a group, if you thought something that showed a right attitude, he would look at you, smile, and then go on talking to other people. Even in big crowds, he would notice our little thoughts. If he would say something that was especially meaningful to you, he'd look at you at that instant, smile, then continue with his talk. He had such a marvelous consciousness that was really in tune with everybody just as if he was in them, because he was in them. He told us sometimes, "I know every single thought that every one of you is thinking." What an incredible claim! Yet he proved it again and again.

Yogananda once said to me, "I have plans for you." I knew that he meant that he wanted to send me to India because he had been talking about going there. I was very pleased because going to India was naturally very exciting to me. Suddenly, after I had left him that day, the thought occurred to me that if I went to India, I wouldn't be near him anymore. I fell into a dark mood of rejection, thinking that I wasn't a good enough disciple to be kept with him, that he was just getting rid of the overflow. I was in a black mood for a couple of days, but finally shook it off by thinking, "He'll only do what's good for me. If he wants me to go, it's because that's what I need, not because he wants to get rid of me." Soon I felt much better. When I saw him again, I was feeling fine. I had told no one about this mood, and when I had seen him last I was feeling perfectly happy. As soon as he saw me, he said, "No more moods now. How will you be able to help others?" He knew what I had been going through.

Again and again he proved this to us. Sometimes he proved it in rather funny ways. One of the disciples wasn't able to follow the rules very well. He worked at the church in Phoenix, and was coming back to Encinitas to see Master. Late one night, as he was driving on the highway, he got hungry, and stopped at a restaurant to eat. It was the only one open, and all they had were hamburgers. Master taught us not to eat meat, especially not beef. He thought to himself, "He won't know," and had a couple of hamburgers. He went happily on to Encinitas, and when he arrived, spoke to Master on the phone. Master didn't make a big thing of his insight, but at the end of the conversation, he said, "Oh, by the way, when you're on the highway late at night, and the only place to eat has nothing but hamburgers, better not eat."

Divine Protection for the Disciple

So many times Yogananda's disciples found themselves divinely protected in ways that were amazing. This same disciple, much as he bent the rules, had great love for Master. On another occasion he was driving along and picked up a hitchhiker, though Master had told us not to do so. The hitchhiker was sitting in back as they were driving along, when suddenly the disciple heard Master's voice say, "He has a knife!" He looked around and sure enough the hitchhiker was poised with a knife about to attack him. The disciple said strongly, "Put that knife down." Tremblingly, the man lowered the knife, and jumped out of the car.

Once another disciple was going down the very steep Mt. Washington hill in a large flat-bed truck. Just as he was about to make the turn, he put his foot on the brake, and his foot went all the way to the floor. There was no resistance to it at all. The brakes had failed. To go right down that slope would have meant death because he would have gone over a steep embankment. Inwardly he asked, "Master, is this what you want?" Immediately the truck came to a stop.

Dr. Lewis had an experience of Master's divine protection once when he was going to a center meeting in Massachusetts. His car skidded on an icy patch just as he was approaching a bridge. Ordinarily he would have slid off the bridge into the freezing water, but he said it felt as though there was a hand on the hood of the car pushing it to a stop.

Miracles happened around Master all the time, but somehow they never seemed particularly important because he didn't want to draw attention to them. He never dwelt on them, because they were not the essence of our life with him.

Another thing I found in living with Master was that people would sometimes say, "Well, I don't think he really knew about this particular area. After all he didn't have this kind of experience; or after all he was an Indian, and we're Americans." I heard it several times from disciples, and every time it was on that point that the disciple fell into delusion and suffered for many years because of it.

I remember a disciple who had met some other spiritual teacher who claimed that he could shut his eyes in meditation on one mountain top, and when he opened them he would be on another peak. I don't think that anybody ever saw him do it, but he made the claim, and this was enough for this disciple. She decided that anybody with all these powers must be great. So she went to Master and said, "I have found another guru that I want to follow." She was not a close disciple, otherwise the bond would have been on a deeper level. He said to her, "Very well then, I withdraw my ray." She had been a shining person, but when she came back a year later, the light in her eyes was gone. She hadn't found anything. Though Master's love was the infinite love of God, he couldn't impose himself on anyone.

An Expression of Compassion to All

His divine love continually reached out to others. A lovely story that another disciple told me about Master took place once when they were out for a drive. As they were traveling along, Master suddenly said, "Stop the car," and went into a little store. To everyone's amazement he busily went about buying all sorts of useless junk. Finally he brought all his selections up to the counter and gave them to the woman there. She totaled the whole thing up, and he paid for it. As soon as she took his money, she burst out crying and said, "I very, very badly need exactly this sum of money to pay my rent today. My child is in the hospital, the store was about to be closed, and I didn't know where I was going to get the money. Now God has sent you here to buy these things so that I could have just what I needed." Such universal compassion that can tune into the sorrow of all people gives us a glimpse of the divine.

He used to walk up and down in front of the bars in Los Angeles, just to send his vibrations to those people and lift them out of their suffering. I know what that power is. I remember once, when I was very new, being out at Twenty-Nine Palms with him. I was lying in my sleeping bag on the floor one night, when all of a sudden I woke up. I felt that God himself was in the room. It was such a powerful vibration that I couldn't even sleep and immediately I began meditating. I looked over and saw one of the other disciples was meditating as well. Then I looked out of the window, and there was Master walking back and forth outside. He was there simply in order to give us his blessings, and to help us to overcome the darkness in ourselves.

God Helping God

I often think to myself with great regret how little I understood him when I was with him. As I grow older and come to appreciate things I had taken for granted, to see his greatness in ways I had overlooked, I wish I had the chance to re-live my years with him. I wish I had a chance to be a better disciple during his lifetime. Yet, I also realize that twenty years from now I'll probably say the same thing about my present state. Until we attain the state of divine union, our ignorance is really unfathomable. The best thing we can do is to just forget ourselves. We're not important. What we want to do is get away from the delusion of being separate from one another. We should try to be the servants of all, and yet understand that it's just God serving God.

I remember an especially sweet episode in our life with Master. He was about to go out, when he stopped some of the monks and said to us, "It's a hot day, isn't it?" We knew what he meant was that he wanted to give us money to buy ice cream. We didn't want to impose on him, so we said, "It's not very hot, sir." He looked at us so sweetly and said, "Are you sure it's not very hot? Perhaps a little bit hot?" Finally we conceded, "Well, sir, if you say so." Then he said, "I can't keep money and I won't. Here's some money for ice cream." He gave us each a dollar, but I used my own money and, to this day, I still have the dollar he gave me.

There was a time when he was having a great deal of difficulty with his legs from taking on the karma of others. He couldn't walk, so we were helping him into the car. Lovingly he said, "You are all so kind to me with your many attentions." We protested, "But sir, it's you who are kind to us!" He smiled at us, then replied, "God is helping God. That's His drama." He never accepted the thought that he was in a position that merited any special consideration. It was all God serving God. He was really the servant of all. He never wanted anything except to give and to serve.

He also saw himself as the friend of everyone—the truest friend that I have ever seen. In spite of all his responsibilities, if he said he would do something for someone, it was always done, no matter how small the request. Once, my mother was coming for a visit, and I asked him if it would be possible for him to see her. I was reluctant to ask because I knew how busy he was, but he said, "Yes, of course." I also asked, "Would you please pray that she come onto this path?" He agreed. It was quite a while before she actually did come, and I thought that he'd probably have forgotten my request with so many other things on his mind. After her visit with him, however, just as she was about to leave, he took hold of her hand and prayed aloud with great intensity that her soul be brought onto this path. I was deeply moved that he would do that for me, that he would remember. It showed me something of his greatness that he could give so much attention to all the requests brought to him.

I think part of his greatness was that he could be so totally conscious in little ways, in small attentions, small consider-ations. He could be so true as a human being, so loyal, and so concerned for the welfare of others. He was the friend of all, so much that you knew that no one you'd ever met was such a friend as he. He said, "When I am gone, only love can take my place." It's that love that resides in the hearts of his devotees. As people become more in tune with him, become better disciples, you can see his love and consciousness growing in their eyes. In a way, it's as if Master was incarnate in all his disciples here.

To Please Him–Serve All

Love and joy are the qualities that manifested most strongly in Yogananda's life. This is what we feel in our attunement with one another—the bond of God loving God, of God serving God. Our gratitude and fulfillment come in the opportunity to be of service to God in one another.

Master showed us the way in this. I remember one incident at Mt. Washington that took place at our Christmas dinner. We had the table all set with place cards for each person. All the places were taken, and food had been cooked for exactly that many people. Suddenly, twenty-five extra people appeared unexpectedly, and twenty-five of us had to give up our seats. Normally you would find people saying, "I don't want to give up my seat." We looked forward all year long to being with Master at the Christmas banquet and hearing him talk afterward. You'd expect people would have fought to keep their seats. At that dinner the only fighting was for the privilege of giving up our seats. When Master heard about that afterward, he said, "These are the things that please me."

This is the way to please Master—to put yourself last, to put yourself behind others. This is the goal, and this is the way that Master taught us. I think that of all the things about him—his great wisdom, his miraculous powers, his *samadhi*—the thing that touches me the most is the sweetness of his humility. There is such inspiration in those things he did for others that are small and unimportant in an outward way, but are, finally, the sum of greatness.

Let us be thankful that we have the life and inspiration of such a master to draw from. He lives with us now. He is in our hearts. He's as much with us today as he was then. All we have to do is to attune ourselves with him, to feel his guidance, to feel his blessings. Again and again since his passing he has shown how very near and very dear he really is.

Questions & Answers
with Swami Kriyananda

Question: Can the guru's grace be transmitted by his disciples after he has passed away?

Kriyananda: I used to believe that my duty as a disciple of a great master was to draw people to him, but thereafter not to "intrude" on the flow of his grace to them. (In the name of devotion, you see, I practiced a kind of spiritual irresponsibility!) But then I saw that there were matters in which new disciples might still draw help from my experience on the path. I rarely, if ever, volunteered suggestions and advice, but when people came to me for help I told them what I could—tentatively always, almost fearfully, still considering my words only an intrusion.

Then in time I came to understand that it is the duty of every disciple to constantly be a channel for his guru's grace. I realized, too, that the flow of that grace depends, not on outward acts of conversion or on intellectual words of advice, but on *an inner sense of divine presence.* The extent to which a person can keep and share this sense of his guru's living presence determines his own trueness to the role of discipleship.

For it is by acting as channels for the divine that the divine blesses us, too. This is the very essence of karma yoga, the path of right, dutiful action.

Master once told me that one must free at least six others before one can be completely freed of all karmic bondage. When his most advanced woman disciple, Sister Gyanamata, died, he remarked to a few of us that she had attained final liberation. As he said that, the question crossed my mind, "But how can she have been liberated, if she had no disciples?" Master, reading my thoughts, replied, "She *had* disciples."

His reply, you see, underscored the truth of what I am saying, that we must all be willing instruments for the blessings of God and guru.

Disciples, moreover, who attain Self-realization will themselves deserve to be called gurus, according to what Master said to me about Sister Gyanamata. But whereas he was the guru of the entire movement that God founded through him, they will be gurus only to limited groups of students, to whom he will always remain the supreme guru.

This is in fact the way these matters are universally understood in India. But in that country many people have taken matters too far. When a great *avatar,* or divine incarnation, is born into this world, he comes with extraordinary power to uplift others. Rarely will even enlightened disciples approach him in that ability. But in India such a great master, after he dies, is often ignored in favor of living disciples who in fact can reflect little more than a fraction of his glory. It would be more fitting for them to be considered always only his instruments. For he does in fact work through them. How perfectly he does so depends on the degree of their own inner attunement, but a great master can work at least minor miracles even through lesser, but faithful, disciples.

Master said that many would find God who were drawn to him after he left this world. He lives now, and acts with varying degrees of power through everyone who is in tune with him as well as blessing anyone who appeals to him directly.

Chapter 5

PARAMHANSA YOGANANDA:
INCARNATION OF
DIVINE LOVE

Words of Paramhansa Yogananda

It is difficult to find one's way out of a labyrinth. When you enter it you may think, 'Oh, I'll find my way out easily, any time I want to.' But each time you think you've found the way out, you are only led into another blind alley. You need what Theseus had—Theseus, of Greek legend, who slew the minotaur. Ariadne gave him a thread to unreel as he was going in. That thread enabled him to retrace his steps back out. That thread symbolizes the Guru's advice, and your inner attunement with him. Even mental attunement will suffice to lead you to freedom. By that sacred thread, you will be led by God's grace.

—*The Essence of Self-Realization: The Wisdom of Paramhansa Yogananda*, by Swami Kriyananda. *See Resources.*

Paramhansa Yogananda: Incarnation of Love
Taken from Talks by Swami Kriyananda

There are many aspects of this one can discuss, but I want to talk especially about the present nature of the divine love which Yogananda embodied—the existence of it right now in this room, in our hearts, and in infinity. Our ignorance may be eons old, and yet the reality of that love is ours forever.

There is a tendency for his disciples to think of him as the things he did or said, and to forget that his true reality even while he was on this earth was not his outer expression. As he often said, "I killed Yogananda long ago. No one dwells in this temple now but God." This was the reality that we would become aware of from time to time when we were with him. We could feel his presence—it was like an emanation coming from his body. We could feel his reality inside us, but when we saw him smile or heard him talk, the tendency was to look at him as that personality.

I remember him saying to me once about entering a new incarnation, "When I have to take on a new personality, it's like putting on a warm overcoat on a hot day. It's uncomfortable, but then I get used to it." He said "take on a personality" because he isn't the personality. If, when looking into his eyes, we were able to get beneath the physical expression we suddenly felt we were gazing into infinity. His eyes were different from most peoples' eyes, not just in their stillness or their love, but in the total absence of ego, of likes and dislikes. When you look into most peoples' eyes, you see the desires for certain things, the aversions toward others. Even when the bonfire of life burns down, there are still those glowing, banked embers of desire. But with Yogananda, it was as if his eyes opened onto infinite vistas.

Yogananda didn't invent divine love, he *manifested* it. We can use him as an example to understand ourselves better, because our human experience of love is so small compared to the infinity of divine love. There's an aspect of this love that most people not only don't take into account, but are almost frightened by.

Sister Gyanamata set a fascinating example in this way. She was one of his closest, and therefore, one must assume, his dearest disciples. I say "dearest" not in the sense of a personal affection, but in the sense that she fulfilled his spiritual expectation of her. He holds this out for each one of us, but that expectation is unfulfilled everyday of our lives in one way or another until we finally come out into the light. Then he can say, "This is my child," as he used to say to Rajarshi and as he felt toward Sister Gyanamata.

She was very ill for the last twenty years of her life. He could have healed her, but he didn't. He could have let her go, because it was her time, but he held on to her. He made a contract with God that she would not go until he released her. Due to her illness, she suffered very much physically, and yet he kept her in that body suffering. You might think, "What kind of love is it that would allow her to suffer?" Yet what is a little bit of suffering if it allows you to attain freedom from all suffering for all eternity? At the end of her life she attained liberation in God.

The Masters Allow Us to Suffer to Find Freedom

This is the kind of love that Master has. We see it reflected in a very limited way by a doctor as he treats his patients. He doesn't want to hurt them, but he knows that through the pain he inflicts, he can free them from greater pain. So what he's really doing is manifesting compassion and love. The same thing is true to a much greater extent of a master who is one with God, or of God Himself through the law of karma. You might think, "What a terrible law God has created with this law of karma that can make it possible for people to suffer to the extent that they do!" When you look at the things people go through—the physical, mental, and spiritual anguish—they're sometimes past imagination.

In the *Bhagavad Gita*, Krishna said to Arjuna, "Get away from *my* ocean of suffering and misery." He says "my" because he created it. Is that a sign of lack of love? To our limited human understanding, it's very easy to believe that it is. Many people have lost faith in God just because of the pain that they or others have endured. Yet the law is set up to help you to turn toward what you really are so that eventually, and it will take as long or short a time as you chose, you will learn where your answers, bliss, and freedom lie. It doesn't come from just living in this dungeon of a world.

If you're a parent and you see your child playing in a mud puddle, what will you do? Will you say, "Oh, what a pity! That's a dirty mud puddle. Let me clean it up for you"? No, you'll pull the child out. God's purpose is to take us out of this mud puddle of suffering, not to improve the world so that it can be a nicer mud puddle. It will still be a dungeon compared to the infinite bliss that is our real destiny.

Yogananda told a story of a frog that lived on the shore of a vast lake. Behind a large sand dune along the shore, the frog heard lots of other frogs croaking. He thought, "Someday I'll go over and see what they're doing over there." Finally he decided to give up his enjoyment of the lake for awhile, and he hopped over the dune. To his amazement he found thousands of frogs gathered around a tiny pond. They were all clambering on each others' backs to get to the water. There was also a frog king at this tiny pond who was proud because he could demand the right to walk on the other frogs' backs. The frog seeing all this thought, "This is terrible!" He hopped down and told some of them all about the beautiful big lake just over the sand dune.

They said, "You sound like a mad man, but we'd better take you to our king. He'll know what to do with you."

So they took him to the king, and he told him all about the large lake.

The frog king said, "That's ridiculous. There can be no larger puddle than this one. Ha, ha, ha, you and your lake. It's impossible." But the frog from the lake kept insisting, until finally they got very angry with him and denounced him as an imposter.

The king said, "Do you mean to say that your lake is, ha, ha, ha, *this* big?" He then jumped a quarter-way across the puddle landing on several other slave frogs as he did so because there was hardly any access to the water.

The frog from the lake said, "Oh, it's much bigger than that."

"You mean to say that your lake dares to be *this* big?" said the frog king, and he jumped half-way across.

The first frog said, "No, it's bigger than a thousand of your little puddles."

Then they were all set to persecute him, to crucify him, and do whatever it is that they could do to silence this frog because he was an embarrassment to the public weal. Yet the truth was that there was enough water in that lake for all of these frogs and for many, many more.

This is the predicament that great masters find themselves in when they come into this world. They come here seeing this as a mud puddle, and their real thrust is to help people to commune with the Infinite. The masters see that out of ignorance, people will attribute every possible wrong motive to them for daring to speak the truth. Yet with compassion, knowing that each soul has to go through the same process, the masters try to show us the way to freedom. If they have to get crucified, they accept it and just come back to try again.

This is the way of the masters. They have an infinite love for people because they know, first of all, that they themselves went through it. Secondly, they know that beneath all our ignorance there is a potential germ of awakening into wisdom. This is their goal—to help us to achieve that awakening.

Now if we didn't have the law of karma, people would go on in their ignorance forever. It's hard work to get rid of all our delusions and finally find that kernel of reality in ourself. The law of karma has to be just as it is, even though you and I don't always like it.

Yogananda gave this illustration to explain it: When you put your hand on a hot stove, it burns you. The next time you know better. But if the stove didn't cause pain, you would leave your hand there and damage your body far more.

So the pains of this world are intended only to help us understand which direction to go. Sometimes we insist on our way and keep going in the wrong direction anyway. Master once said, "Stalin will suffer for 100,000 years for the karma that he accrued in this lifetime."

Debi Mukerji, a disciple of Yogananda, asked, "Only 100,000 years?"

Master replied, "How long do you want?"

Man wants others to suffer for eternity, but God doesn't want that. He loves all. He loves Stalin just as much as He loves Jesus Christ or Krishna, because He loves Himself—the divine consciousness—in all.

But we do have lessons to learn if we go the wrong way. There is that aspect to a great master's life that is not easy to understand because they express divine, not human, love. Their love is not for our bodies or our personalities, nor for our earthly convenience. I saw many disciples looking to Master for ego approval, but he would not respond to that kind of energy. When disciples looked at him with that desire, I saw him just look back calmly as though it was their higher self looking at them.

The Ego is Frightened by the Power of Divine Love

There is this aspect to divine love that is quite honestly frightening to the ego. As the sleepless saint in the *Autobiography of a Yogi* said, "My rule of non-availability is not for my sake but for that of other people."

People find it inconvenient to be around a master because his insights level their egos. It's just not convenient to be around somebody who can instantly see through your games. In the early years of Master's work at Mt. Washington, it was like a hotel—people checking in and out all the time. You'd think, "Gosh, with this great master, they'd all want to stay here and lap it up." But many didn't stay because it wasn't so easy when he started giving them not milk and honey but vinegar. He was very outspoken—gentle in one way, but very strong in another.

This power aspect of divine love is not merely a sweet sentiment. When I would look into Master's eyes and feel that love, tears would flow down my cheeks, because it was so moving, so uplifting, so reassuring to realize that *that* is who

I was. Yet that same love could scold, though it was never with anger.

There's a lovely story in *The Path* where Jean Haupt was sitting at one end of the room and a woman disciple was at the other. Master was scolding her, striding up and down the room shouting. You'd have thought he was furious with her, but he was like a parent trying to scold his child in order to impress a lesson on her. Every time Master turned his back to her, he looked at Jean, winked and smiled, then turned back to his scolding. But he was never angry—he didn't have it in him to be angry.

This power is an aspect of divine love that I want you to understand, because it is something you must live with now. Don't think that if God gives you tests and difficulties He doesn't love you. The truth is, the more he loves you, the more quickly he will give you these things to free you from suffering forever.

So be grateful for whatever He gives you. Don't think, "Oh, God, why are you doing this to me?" You know why. He wants to get you out of his ocean of misery, and through the power of divine love break forever the chains that hold you in delusion.

When people read *Autobiography of a Yogi* they sometimes think of Master as being only sweet, and the power of his personality is not always understood. That's why it's always a shock when people hear a recording of his voice for the first time. His voice was very powerful, as you know if you've heard him say, "I, Paramhansa Yogananda, am singing to you." Even though there were times when the way he talked would melt your heart with sweetness, yet you could feel behind that voice such power and bliss that it was an inspiration to listen to. I couldn't begin to share this inspiration with you because the very tone of his voice expressed that power.

Yet we mustn't dwell on the days when he lived as if they were his only reality. Don't think, "Oh, how wonderful it was then," but remember that he lives right now. There is a beautiful story that happened a few years ago to the mother of one of the residents at Ananda while she was visiting there. She was walking in one of the meadows in the community, and had a vision of Yogananda. He spoke with her for a long time, and answered many questions that she put to him. (This all took place in Spanish since she speaks very little English.) Finally she asked him, "Do you come here often?"

Yogananda answered, "I'm here all the time." For several hours after this experience she was in a state of deep upliftment and was unable to speak.

He *is* here all the time. You can feel his presence in this room, while you know at the same time he is omnipresent. He's no more in one place than another, and yet there are certain foci of that divine energy.

He told us once, "I have meditated in every spot of Mt. Washington." When we went to Lake Shrine for the first time, he had us put on our swimming suits and go out into the water. Then he said, "I'm sending the divine light into this water. From now on this is holy water."

You, too, are a focus for his presence. What greater manifestation of the divine can there be than through a human being? Once Master told Dr. Lewis that when a soul is liberated, his family also becomes liberated for seven generations backwards and forwards. He clarified this by saying they are not *fully* liberated, but their evolution is greatly speeded up so that they reach a high plane of consciousness after death. Then Dr. Lewis asked Master, "What about the disciples?"

Master replied, "Oh, they come first." So you see, it's the same thing—seven generations of disciples are liberated, too. For those of us who are his direct disciples, we're the first generation, and you all are the next. Actually it goes on much more than just seven generations of disciples. The power of Buddha is alive in Buddhists today, just as the power of Jesus is alive in Christians today.

The Masters Are Uncompromising for our Welfare

There are aspects even in the life of an incarnation of love such as Yogananda that were difficult to understand because they were challenging and absolutely uncompromising. Jean Haupt, a direct disciple, told a story he'd heard about a man who wanted to be accepted as a disciple. Master said that this man had been with Sri Yukteswar and had reincarnated, but he wouldn't allow him to join. Jean told me that finally this man pleaded with Master quite poignantly, yet still he said harshly, "Absolutely not. Never." You wouldn't expect that, would you?

Remember the story in *Autobiography of a Yogi* when that man wanted to join Babaji's band, but he told him that he wasn't karmically ready. In desperation the man said he would jump off a precipice if he wasn't accepted, and Babaji said impersonally, "Jump then." His total commitment, as shown by his jumping off the cliff, purified him enough for Babaji to bring him back to life and include him in his band. But what if it hadn't? Would you say then that Babaji had been cruel? In this example we see the love which was the reason behind the disciple. What if that reason had been buried by the fact that this man still wasn't ready even after committing that sacrifice? Would you then say, "Oh, what a cruel master"? Not at all.

Whenever a master seems to punish anyone, they do it out of love with the ultimate purpose of freeing that person.

It's like the story of the great Tibetan yogi, Milarepa, who had to go through intense suffering and trials eight times before he was purified enough to receive initiation from his guru. What if he had given up after six periods of testing? He'd just have to come back and do it again. Then people would have said, "What a cruel guru to allow that to happen!" But we must understand there is *never* cruelty in divine love. There *is* power, and that power stays with you and changes you forever.

Sister Gyanamata told the story of a guru who disciplined his disciples by throwing bricks at them. They all fled like ducks before a hunter. One disciple, however, picked up one of the bricks with great devotion and took it home with him because he felt it was a blessing. "My guru has chosen to treat me this way," he thought, "and what he's given me has to be a sign of his grace." When he got home he found that the brick had turned to gold.

This is an example of what the spiritual path is all about. Don't think that Master expresses his love for you especially when he gives you nice things, which he does also. Treasure even more the fact that he takes enough pains with you to give you difficult experiences because it's those, above all, that will help you to grow.

If you want to become free in this lifetime, then be a warrior. Don't be a beggar grasping for a little penny at the gates of heaven. When a Master comes into this world, whatever he does is a blessing. Even when he seems to be giving a blow, he's giving a blessing.

There was a person once to whom Master gave divine love, and this person turned against him. He commented to me, "When you go against divine love, you crucify yourself." He said that this man had crucified himself by that action, and had to go through great suffering. Yet Master didn't wish that suffering upon him—rather by going through that suffering a lesson came to him on a much deeper level.

There was someone who struck Master publicly, and his hand was paralyzed for six months afterwards. Did Master say, "I throw my thunderbolt at you"? Not at all. It's just that when you go against that love, you go against the divine law. It's like a wire that doesn't have insulation around it—if you touch it you get shocked. If you hurt a saint, then naturally you'll get more of a shock that way. So this persons' hand was paralyzed, but that, too, was a blessing.

When you get that power from God, even if it hurts you or destroys your body, it's still divine power. It will sink into your soul and give you blessings that might otherwise take many incarnations to achieve.

Have Faith in the Power and Constant Presence of Divine Love

When a Master is born into this world, he sheds great power and love—not just sweetness. In that love is the power to liberate, to destroy delusion, to uplift you into the one truth of which you are a manifestation no matter how you live. To understand how many lives you must pass through before you even begin to think of God, all you have to do is walk down the street and see people whose minds are nowhere near that. They wouldn't know what you are talking about. To have any real contact with divine love, to be blessed by that power even if it hurts temporarily, will bless you more than you can imagine. Have faith in this truth.

I'm not trying to dogmatize you. I'm simply saying, "By their fruits, ye shall know them."

Look at the lives of saints. You'll see that of every one who has found God, not one has said, "What a scam."

They don't. They all say, "Everything that we've endured was worth it."

There's a lovely story that Master enjoyed telling of St. Teresa of Avila, who even though she endured a great deal of physical suffering throughout her life, served God unceasingly. Even at the end of her life she was still dedicated to serving Christ and starting new monasteries and convents. One day at the end of her life when she was quite old and couldn't even walk, she was being carried on a litter to found a new convent.

They came to a stream which was in flood, and in trying to ford the stream the horse they put her on lost its footing and was swept away. She was swept away with it into the turbulent water, and was given up as drowned. Suddenly she found herself on the opposite bank exhausted and soaking. Jesus appeared before her and said with great love, "Don't feel bad, Teresa. This is how I treat all my friends."

Teresa, ever with a ready wit, replied, "Ah, my Lord, that is why you have so few." So we must stiffen our spine a bit.

We've been talking of the two aspects of divine love of which Master was an incarnation. The first is the *power* and *rightness* of that love—that whatever happens is always the right thing for you. But the next thing is the *constant presence* of that love. It's not something that was expressed only long ago. It's something that you carry with you right now. What you need to do is make it more and more dynamic to your present awareness. Don't think, "Oh, how lucky those people were to live with him."

In my years of building Ananda, I have never said, "I lived with him. Don't you think I should know?" I *did* live with him and I *should* know, but I don't want to put it on that level. You're the one who must recognize truth within yourself. If you don't, then what does it matter what I say? I try to appeal to that in you that will recognize this. That's how Master taught, and that's how we must live.

Don't think in terms of *then*, but live in the thought that he is living with us *right now*. He is in this room, and above all, he's in your heart.

Chapter 6

The Guru as
Divine Friend

Words of Paramhansa Yogananda

"The bond with the guru, once established, is not for one lifetime only. It is forever. Even after the disciple has attained spiritual freedom, he acknowledges the guru as the channel through which his liberation came.

"For the guru is simply a channel for God's power and wisdom. God is the true Guru.

"The guru is like a transformer, which makes a higher voltage of electricity available to ordinary households.

"Sometimes, indeed, the disciple becomes greater than the guru. Such was the case with Jesus, who was more spiritually developed than John the Baptist, although John the Baptist–as I explain in my autobiography*–was his guru from former incarnations. This was why John said, in humility, that Jesus ought to be baptizing him. And it was why Jesus replied, 'Suffer it to be so now: for thus it becometh us to fulfill all righteousness.' (Matthew 3:14, 15) It was also why Jesus said, 'Among those that are born of women there is not a greater prophet than John the Baptist.' (Luke 7:28) Wasn't Jesus himself born of woman? He was giving recognition, simply, to the fact that his debt as a disciple was eternal.

"Thus, you see, the bond of guru and disciple is not that of master and slave. It is an eternal bond of divine love and friendship.

"If, in the beginning, the guru disciplines his disciple, it is as that disciple's best and truest friend; as one who would help him to achieve what he most wants in his soul. Only a false guru would pamper his disciples' egos with flattery.

"A true guru never disciplines with selfish motivation. Whatever teaching or discipline he gives to the disciple comes not from himself, but from God."

—*The Essence of Self-Realization: The Wisdom of Paramhansa Yogananda*, by Swami Kriyananda. See Resources.

The Guru as Divine Friend

Excerpted from *Religion in the New Age*, by Swami Kriyananda (essay originally titled "Why I Love My Guru, Paramhansa Yogananda").

Friendship, Yogananda used to say, is the most rewarding human experience because it is a free gift, without any compulsion. Even in mother's love a certain compulsion exists: the compulsion of nature in the thought that her children are *her own*. Were some child of hers to die and be reborn next door, would she feel the same love for it? Not possessive love, certainly.

Noble an "institution" as friendship is, however, it was not until I met my Guru that I came to understand its higher octaves. As a divine friend he was perfection itself. For friendship should be uplifting, and that is something it is not, always. So long as a relationship is between two egos, it may only reinforce ego-consciousness.

Much can be said, all the same, in favor of ordinary human friendship, even when it only affects the ego. Experiments have been done on plants showing that when a plant is given love it flourishes, whereas if love is denied it, its growth becomes stunted by comparison. Moreover, if hate and rejection are directed at it, it often withers and dies. Friendship is like that. Even if it offers only ego-balm, a healthy ego is much more to be desired than a crippled, sickly one, forever unsure of itself, inwardly wilting, and cringing before everything and everybody.

Though much, then, might be said of the possible negative influences of ordinary human friendship, basically it is something all human beings need.

I have in this life been fortunate in many respects, but perhaps in none of them so much as in two inborn qualities: first, never to be influenced in my opinions of others by what they thought of me; and second, never to feel even tempted to justify myself (not to myself either) when I knew I was in the wrong. These qualities have been my strength. True friendship must spring not from need, but from inner strength; only in this way can it be purely giving.

One danger of friendship lies in the fact that friends *want* you to agree with them. Bad friends, consequently, want you to agree with and support them in error. As my Guru put it, "If you try to talk to them of higher things, they reply jovially, 'Oh, get off it! Come have a drink!'" This is *friendship*?

Too often, in other words, a person's apparent friends are actually enemies to his highest interests. As the Bhagavad Gita puts it, "When the self is the friend of the Self, it is its greatest friend. But when the self is the enemy of the Self, it is its greatest enemy."

A true friend is one who helps you to befriend that higher Self. He supports everything that is best and truest for your highest welfare. He sympathizes with you, and tries to understand your point of view. He will not condemn you hastily for any disagreement, nor separate himself from you in his sympathy owing to any divergence of opinion. There are both dignity and mutual respect in such a relationship, and, yes, a shared sense of fun also. For an ability to laugh kindly together is one way of sharing trust, confidence, and mutual support.

I hadn't the advantage in my childhood and youth of many close friendships, for I was never in one place long enough to form them. I did live till I was nine in Teleajen (Romania), but childhood friendships are not often deep, and many of my friends lived there just as temporarily as we did, until their fathers were shifted further by their company. I spent a year and a half in Switzerland, where I was ill most of the time. Six months followed in Bucharest, and then two years at school in England. We moved to America in 1939, where I spent a year at Hackley School near Tarrytown, New York; two years at Kent School in Connecticut; a year at Scarsdale High; two years at Haverford College; a year and a half at Brown University; a year in Charleston, South Carolina; and then—Master and SRF (fourteen years with the latter; sixty years, so far, with the former).

Rod, my best friend in college, had a twofold influence on me: one for the good, the other for the not so good. He helped me to regain my self-confidence when I needed it. Unfortunately, though brilliant, he had the fault of intellectual pride, by which he infected me. My intellect being perhaps my strong point, it also became my weak link.

Through all the years that followed, my one truest and best of all possible friends was always my Guru, Paramhansa Yogananda. He was true in *every* respect: the human quite as much as the divine. It's true that I couldn't joke with him in the familiar way friends enjoy with one another. Though I couldn't altogether repress my sense of humor with him,

I was too young not to be always in deep awe of him. For me, being with him was like being in the presence of God Himself. Yet I asked him endless questions—more, perhaps, than anyone else. And he answered me, for he *wanted* me to understand. Again, if *he* joked with *me*, I, with my lively sense of humor, would joke back. Yet I couldn't help holding him at a certain distance, never quite sure of myself in his presence.

That much said, he was with me *not at all* the kind of stern disciplinarian he has sometimes been described as being. He was kind, forgiving, endlessly and deeply understanding, supportive of all my (indeed, of everyone's) human feelings and failings—not, indeed of the failings themselves, but of *us*, as people. I found him to be ever anxious to help us in our efforts to mature and to grow out of our every delusion.

Once he scolded me for my involvement in a confrontation where I had felt righteously indignant. It took me a little while to adjust mentally to this *volte-face* of being scolded for (as I saw it) doing right, but I said to him the next day, "Please, Master, scold me more often." Looking at me deeply, with heartfelt understanding, he answered, "I understand, but that isn't what you need. You need more devotion."

He also encouraged me in every little gain; often, no one else even noticed him doing so. One day he said to me lovingly, "Keep on with your devotion, Walter. Just see how dry your life is, when you depend on intellect."

And one time, feeling intensely my separation from him, I went to Encinitas, where he had gone for a visit, on purpose to see him. As soon as we met, he responded kindly, "I have missed you, Walter." That evening, David Smith (a brother disciple) involved us in worldly chatter, and my devotion slipped.

When I saw Master the next day, he tugged at a lock of my hair lightly, and reminded me with the same loving smile (though with a hint of reproof), "I have missed you."

It pains me when I hear people say coldly, "*Master* wouldn't have approved of that! *Master* wouldn't tolerate disorder! *Master* was always a strict taskmaster!" These things have been said to justify the disciple's own lack of kindness, sympathy, and simple humane charity. But I remember one time (I've quoted it elsewhere in these essays) when he came into the monks' dining room and found it in utter, embarrassing chaos. His only comment then was, "Well, it might be worse!"

In his treatment of the other disciples, I never saw him speak to them harshly. In fact, I wonder whether their impression of harshness didn't come from their own rebellious egos. The few times he scolded me, I saw only regret in his eyes for having to speak strongly to me. He did so for my benefit, purely.

There was a period in Daya's discipleship, she told me, when he scolded her almost daily. She resented it, especially because his manner was then so different from what he had shown her when she first came. One evening she prayed, "From now on, Divine Mother, I will direct my love first to You." When she went indoors for his blessing, he tapped her lightly on the top of her head and murmured approvingly, "Very good." The scoldings stopped. He had wanted to break her of an excessively human attachment to him.

With those who were not disciples he was affability itself: kindly, warm, entirely accepting, and forgiving of any insult or calumny. I remember one time (I mentioned this occasion in my book, *The Path*) at a public function, a man from India was a bit tipsy and treated Master with a familiarity no one else would have ever dreamed of: putting his arms around Master, laughing jovially, and talking familiarly. Debi, a Bengali disciple, ridiculed the man to Master in Bengali (a language unknown to this Indian) for his inebriation. "Don't!" Master scolded him quietly, so that the man himself wouldn't notice. Master saw this man in the full dignity of a human being, not as someone who, in his drunkenness, had lost that dignity.

Another time the Master, as he was entering a hotel, was approached by a drunken stranger who embraced him and cried, "Hello, Jeshush Chrisht!"

"Hello," Master responded affably, then shared with him a touch of the inner bliss he himself was experiencing. "Shay! What're *you* drinkin'?" demanded the man.

"I can tell you, it has a lot of kick in it!" the Master replied. He then touched this man on the forehead, leaving him sober though perhaps somewhat bewildered.

These are stories I have shared before elsewhere. Here is another one. A member of the Indian community came to Mt. Washington with Ambassador Binay R. Sen just days before Master left his body. This Indian lived in Los Angeles and had devoted years to persecuting the Master by spreading untruths against him. At a certain moment that afternoon the two of them were briefly alone together. Master said to the man, "Remember, I will always love you." Herbert Freed, a brother disciple, overheard the Master's words. A photograph of Master taken at that moment shows the visitor's expression; it reveals a mixture of emotions: wonder, shame, perhaps dismay at his own pettiness. For those who understand the inwardness of that moment, it is a dramatic photograph. (It was this episode, incidentally, that gave me the inspiration for my one-act play, *The Jewel in the Lotus*.)

The Master simply accepted people as they were, with never a breath of criticism, but always with love. It often surprised me to see the completeness of his acceptance. People whom I myself might have turned away from with distaste, Master treated kindly and with a gentle, though always dignified, smile.

Not everyone understood him, by any means. I'll never forget a neighbor of the Master's at Twenty-Nine Palms, when that man gave one of my brother disciples his view. Master used to share fruits with him, an act of generosity that, to this man, seemed beyond comprehension. One day he said, speaking of Master, "You know, he's a little [making a circular movement to indicate someone a little 'tetched' in the head], but," he added admiringly, "he's got a heart of gold!"

The Master was a true friend to everybody, seeing all as his very own. That is why, wherever he went, he always found people friendly and eager to help him.

Yet, when someone came to him and asked to be accepted as a disciple, he saw his responsibility *as a divine friend* to be the highest type of friend he could be to that person. In this sense he might be compared to a divine fisherman: never letting the line get too tight, but if it slackened, testing it to see how forcefully he could reel it in without letting it break.

He was infinitely kind to us, forgiving, supportive, gentle, humorous, one with us in friendship, and ever completely loving. Yet he was also careful, always, to turn our minds and aspirations toward our own highest potential in God. Never did I see him come down from that high purpose. And always in his calm gaze I saw a complete absence of ego-motive, including the slightest impulse either to act or react personally. People—men perhaps especially—who lack personal motivation are often misunderstood by others, bound as almost all people are by personal desires. Master had many self-styled enemies who fancied they saw in him someone dark, someone scheming for subtle, hidden ends which he was not frank enough to admit openly, and which must therefore (so they imagined) have been all the more sinister. I think it was his very strength they feared.

Their fears, however, were nothing but projections of a darkness in their own natures. Perhaps it was his strength, also, that made some of the disciples think of him as harsh. Otherwise, I can't imagine how anyone saw him as anything but a strong bulwark, supportive always of our true needs. No, I think those disciples, too, simply hadn't the humility or the sensitivity to see in him the truest divine friend they would or could ever have.

Only consider his poem, "God's Boatman." In that poem he promised to come back, "if need be a trillion times, as long as one stray brother sits weeping by the wayside." Think of it! There was no personal necessity for him to return to this material plane. He came here out of a purely selfless desire to bring others out of delusion, and lead them back to God's kingdom. How many times, I have often wondered, has he returned to earth already in perfect freedom? I have good reason to believe he has been coming back for many thousands of years, and always with the same purpose, and with the same universal love. He himself often told us, "I killed Yogananda long ago. Only God lives in this temple now." And I heard him declare also, "I was freed many lifetimes ago." Think of it!

The vast majority of souls who achieve oneness with God are satisfied never to emerge from that blissful state again. Divine Bliss is too perfectly satisfying to them, and they suffered enough before attaining it. All they want, now, is eternal, complete rest in the Lord. What did our Guru want from us? Nothing! Nothing, that is, but *our* highest good. Could any friend be more perfect, more dear, more wonderful than that?

When I met him, he said to me, "I give you my unconditional love." No treasure could be greater, surely, than that sacred promise! He has fulfilled it in countless ways. More and more through the years, I have found him mentally guiding me, leading me toward final, inner freedom, filling me with inner bliss.

He hasn't made the way easy—unless, indeed, I consider (as I do) that every hardship has become, in the end, a supernal blessing. No, I can think of no experience in my life that has not ended in sweetness, in an expansion of love, and in deep gratefulness. Forgiveness for wrongs, hurts, betrayals, tests? All I can say is, *what* tests? *what* betrayals? *what* hurts? *what* wrongs? They were never wrongs, personally, *to me*.

In all my dealings with Master in the body, I always knew he was on my side: not *against* anyone or anything else, but supportive of me in all my struggles toward perfection. He responded supportively to my least thought. If I was wrong, he said so in such a way that only I (if others were present) could know what he was talking about. He never blurted out anything. All his words were carefully measured so as to be as understandable and acceptable to me as possible. There was, as I said, a dignity about him that was completely innate and natural. He was, indeed, a king among men, and I think most people felt it instinctively. And everything I ever saw him do or heard him say was completely *appropriate* to the occasion.

Tara (a sister disciple) once remarked to me about him, "Every time I think I've understood him, I find he's much more than that." I didn't say so to her, but I was astonished that anyone could even *think* of understanding him! To me it seemed like trying to "understand" the ocean. His friendship for each of us was deeply personal, yet he was, for each of us, like a window onto infinity, inviting us to "come outside" and merge in that vastness.

I love my Guru, as he himself wrote about his own guru Swami Sri Yukteswar, "as the spoken voice of silent God." He was ever, and is now more than ever, my nearest, dearest companion. If I am right, I feel his inner smile. If I am wrong, I feel his inner encouragement to do better.

He is *on my side* in every struggle against delusion. Could anyone be a better, truer friend than that?

Addendum
This will be brief.

Yesterday, someone who had just read my essay on my love for my Guru suggested to me, "It would be wonderful if you would write further articles on each of Master's outstanding qualities."

I disagreed, for as I pointed out, "Master was *beyond* all qualities: *triguna rahitam*, beyond all the three *gunas*, or qualities, especially as they are expressed in human nature." To describe even his friendship for us as a *quality* is, in the highest sense of the term, a misnomer. His friendship for us is God's love, channeled through that human vehicle. Our love for Master himself must be not only for him personally, but above all for *God through him.*

One time Norman, a brother disciple, wrote Master a note that said, "When I see you, I see only Divine Mother in you." Master, who was humility itself, might have disclaimed his own unworthiness of such a comparison. Instead, he quietly replied, "Then behave accordingly."

For this reason I asked that my letter be withdrawn from *In Divine Friendship* (a book of my letters) concerning a quality of Master's: his enormous will power. I had described that as the foremost of his qualities in which, it seems to me, all of his disciples share. I withdrew that letter because I realized, later, that it wasn't adequate. What *true* disciples share is something much deeper, and perhaps not even something that can be put into words: a subtle attunement with his special *ray* of the Divine Consciousness.

Several people have told me, or have written to say, that, as I feel toward Master, so they feel toward me. I had a dream last night which may help to clarify that thought. I won't relate the dream itself, as it was personal, but I took it as a warning from Master to pass on to all of you.

The essential difference between attunement with Master and attunement with me is that Master lives eternally in cosmic consciousness, whereas I am still struggling to reach that state. What he channels to us is the Infinite Lord Himself. What I am able to channel to you is whatever I have succeeded so far in experiencing within myself of Master's consciousness. That I feel his bliss is a cause of deep gratitude for myself. But I feel it is very important for everyone to realize that whatever I have to give anyone is *not, and must never become, personal.* To the extent that anyone takes it as such it can be binding not only for that person, but also, potentially, for me.

Therefore I plead with you—for my own sake quite as much as for yours: "See me *only* as a channel for our Guru." I try my best to serve you in that capacity, and am grateful if, to any extent, I succeed in that effort. If, however, I seem to be for some of you—if only by default!—the best instrument you've found during your search, please always remember for what, and for whom, this instrument lives. I have no other desire than to bring you closer to God by bringing you into deeper spiritual attunement with my Guru.

He is our actual, ever-living channel to God.

Please never forget this important distinction. And please always remember it in your own dealings with others who come to Master through you, if they seek you out for inspiration and guidance.

PART TWO

Taking the Step of Discipleship

Chapter 7

A New Dispensation

Words of Paramhansa Yogananda

GOD'S BOATMAN

A poem by Paramhansa Yogananda

I want to ply my boat, many times,
Across the gulf-after-death,
And return to earth's shores
From my home in heaven.
I want to load my boat
With those waiting, thirsty ones
Who are left behind:
And carry them by the opal pool
Of iridescent joy—
Where my Father distributes
His all-desire-quenching liquid peace.
Oh! I will come again and again!
Crossing a million crags of suffering,
With bleeding feet, I will come—
If need be, a trillion times—
As long as I know
One stray brother is left behind.
I want Thee, O God,
That I may give Thee to all!
I want salvation,
That I may give it to all!
Free me, then, O God

From the bondage of the body—
That I may show others
How they can free themselves!
I want Thine everlasting happiness,
Only that I may share it with others—
That I may show all my brothers
The way to happiness,
Forever and forever, in Thee.

—*Whispers from Eternity,* Paramhansa Yogananda, edited by Swami
Kriyananda. *See Resources.*

A New Dispensation

By Swami Kriyananda

Published in 1982

I have a discovery to share with you: something exciting. In fact, wonderful. It's a discovery I've come upon not in
a sudden flash, but gradually, with a growing sense of awe,
over a period of many years.

I touched on this discovery in my book, *The Path.* [as
of 2009, the revised title is *The New Path—Ed.]* In a chapter
titled "God Protects His Devotees," I stated: "In the almost
thirty years [as of 1982—*Ed.*] that I have been on this path
[of Self-Realization], I cannot recall to mind a single instance
where a disciple of Paramhansa Yogananda has failed to find
protection in time of real need. Considering the length of time
involved, and thousands of disciples I have known during this
period, this is quite an amazing record." My reference in that

chapter, backed with example after example, was to protection in the face of danger.

Well, over the six years since I wrote that book I've realized that my claim, startling though many a reader must have found it, barely scratched the surface. Much more than protection is involved: divine power; increasing inner security and joy; freedom from mental and emotional delusions; an ability to ride the storms of destiny instead of being driven by them helplessly; a sense of belonging at last—*meaningfully* so—in the universal scheme of things.

In what has often been described as an age of alienation and loneliness, how wonderful to find a way out that is at the same time a way *in*—into deeper attunement with life, with love, with one's fellowman, with God!

"A Special Dispensation"

I first noticed this extraordinary blessing while living as a monk at Mt. Washington (the international headquarters of Self-Realization Fellowship), and serving as a minister at the SRF church on Sunset Blvd., Hollywood: Those who took up this path earnestly came, in time, to manifest a kind of inner radiance that I'd never beheld in anyone else. What I saw was a kindness in their eyes, an inward joy. Everyone they met found it inspiring.

Were these changes, I wondered, simply the fruit of meditation? of sharing with others on the path? of reawakened faith in God? At first I could only ask the questions.

Years later, in 1967, after founding Ananda World Brotherhood Village, I began to observe once again the same phenomenon: Visitors who took up this path earnestly changed in ways that seemed out of all proportion to the time they spent in meditation. Sometimes in hardly a week, traces of tension and worry would begin to vanish; inner joy, to appear. Of Ananda members I remember a visitor once remarking, "Normally, to meet even *one* such person would be enough to make one's whole day. But here, everywhere I look I see people with this power to 'make my day'!"

For many years I've traveled the world, and almost everywhere I've met followers of this path. Always the story has been the same.

Paramhansa Yogananda often said, "This is a special dispensation." More and more, over the years, I've come to realize what a wealth of divine promise he had packed into that simple statement!

Attunement

Over the years, too, I've made a few specific observations:

• For one, that those who serve this work selflessly are those also who gain the most from it;

• That those, again, who try to share with others the light they receive gain more, spiritually, than those who keep it to themselves. (As Paramhansa Yogananda said, "The instrument is blessed by that which flows through it.");

• That they gain the most who seek attunement with others more advanced than they themselves are on the path;

• And that they gain the most, finally, who realize that soul-attunement with this path is more important even than long hours spent in meditation, without the companion effort to establish such inner attunement.

The Divine Ray

I remember in this context a certain woman disciple of this path, a resident of the SRF community in Encinitas. The chief impression she made on me was the joy and peace that she radiated.

One day she approached our guru with the news, "I'm leaving this path. I've found another guru."

"Very well," the Master replied respectfully. "I withdraw my ray."

A year later she returned for a visit. To our sorrow, the joy and peace in her eyes were no longer there. She looked like any other worldly person, asleep to higher realities.

Her example helped me to realize the truth of what our guru often implied in his talks with us: that, through our connection with him, we were affiliated with an actual ray of divine power, a power far transcending even such great blessings as true teachings, scientific meditation techniques, and the saintly example of a great master of yoga. Paramhansa Yogananda would tell his students, "You are not connected with a mere organization, but with the divine power flowing through a line of Self-realized masters." Again he would repeat, "This work is a special dispensation, sent from God."

Inner proof of the truth of his assertion came to me easily: The more I attuned myself to the divine grace flowing through him, the more everything in my own life flowed smoothly. The opposite proved true also: Whenever I sought to progress spiritually by personal efforts alone, without this attunement, I found myself gradually bogging down.

Gradually, too, the objective evidence—as in the case of that woman disciple—mounted. And now that I've been a disciple for over forty years, I can say it with conviction: A special ray of divine grace definitely flows into the lives of those who embrace this path of Self-Realization sincerely.

A Way Out

I've described this truth as a personal discovery. But that doesn't make it new! In fact, it is an ancient teaching, taught in one way or another in every religion: Without grace from above, no way exists for man to escape from delusion. All I've added to this teaching is the conviction born of personal experience.

To understand this truth, imagine yourself in the middle of a large, dark building at night. The floor is littered with countless obstacles, and broken in many places. At every break is a deep hole. Without some kind of light, wouldn't it be very difficult to get safely out of the building?

Again, imagine yourself prisoner in a labyrinth—its maze hopelessly complex, every promising new passageway leading at last, after many turns, to a dead end. In the Greek saga of Theseus, Ariadne gave Theseus a thread to unwind before he entered the labyrinth to fight the Minotaur. Without such a thread, he would never have found his way out.

Now consider how infinitely more complex than any building, or the most intricate labyrinth imaginable, is the human mind!

Divine grace, like a ray of light, pierces the darkness of this world. By rising upon that ray, and only by rising upon it, we can escape from delusion. Like Ariadne's thread, this ray of grace is our subtle tie to Higher Reality. By following it we can trace our way back out of our mind's labyrinth into soul-freedom.

Divine grace, again, like electricity, flows through channels. As electricity is passed on through transmitting stations,
so also is grace: through the attunement of living persons.

In one of the most fascinating passages of his autobiography, Paramhansa Yogananda wrote, "Thoughts are universally
and not individually rooted." (p. 159) His statement is decep-
tively simple. Let us probe it more deeply, by means of
a visualization exercise.

Imagine mighty rivers of consciousness flowing through
the universe—sweeping through vast stellar systems, engulf-
ing planets, catching up in swirling currents the little thoughts,
ideas, and passions of men. In various lands of Earth, and at
various times through the course of history, one cosmic river
or another will touch human lives, perhaps changing thereby
the very course of history.

Men imagine that it is they who create history. As well
might the little leaf, bobbing lightly on the water's surface,
think to determine the river's course! Free will does indeed
exist, but not as most people imagine—not, that is to say, in
private, egoic isolation from the universe. Freedom must be
sought, rather, in broader realities. Man is free only in the sense
that he can choose his influences. Each one can determine
which, out of an infinity of streams of universal consciousness, he will enter.

The rivers of history are extraordinarily powerful. The
great majority of men and women, failing to tune in to
them consciously, are swept helplessly, hither and yon, by
the merest ripples. Geniuses, on the other hand, may—and
saints invariably do—flow serenely and joyously with the
flood until they reach the ocean of cosmic consciousness and

freedom from all bondage. Ordinary man, caught up in fads of the moment, drifts passively more often than not into stagnant by-waters, from which death alone rescues him at last. Instead of the freedom claimed by him as his inalienable human "right," he achieves mere bondage to outwardness, and to ego.

Those, however, who attune themselves to these great streams of consciousness achieve greatness themselves. This is true of genius. It is even truer of spiritual greatness. As the Bible puts it, "As many as *received* him, to them gave he the *power* to become the sons of God." (John 1:12)

Into this valley of the shadow of death—Earth's sorrowful realm—God from time to time, through the agency of one of His awakened Sons, sends the ray of light that I have described. Many are the rays that He has sent throughout history. Salvation is achieved by those who, recognizing their own affinity with one such ray, attune themselves to it, and allow it to lead them out of darkness into the infinite Light. As Jesus put it, "I am the light of the world: he that followeth me shall not walk in darkness, but shall have the light of life." (John 8:12) He spoke here not in personal reference to his humanity, but as a conscious instrument of the infinite Light.

Many, as I say, are the rays of divine light that God has sent into the world. Each has its own special qualities. Those devotees who tune into a particular ray will reflect its qualities in their own lives. As Paramhansa Yogananda put it, "All of Krishna's soldiers were like Krishna."

Thus, all the members of the family of Self-Realization reflect in their lives those qualities which are particular to this special ray of divine grace: kindness (as I mentioned before), and joy; openness, trust, and a certain inner radiance.

The Present Ray

Into this country, and at this particular time in history, God has sent a powerful ray of His light. To see this ray only in terms of Paramhansa Yogananda's personal life and teachings would be to misunderstand the true greatness of his mission. The disciples of Jesus, similarly, have done him a disservice in too much personalizing his mission. The secret of Yogananda's greatness lay in the clarity of his transmission of a new ray of light from the divine. As many as receive it, *and in proportion as they receive it,* to them (as he told his students) will be given the power "to become the sons of God."

"When the Disciple is Ready"

What causes a divine ray to shine down from time to time onto this dark planet? Yogananda's answer to that was, "God chooses those who choose Him." He also said, "He replies to us in proportion to the intensity of our call to Him." Any individual who calls earnestly enough will receive a divine response. That cosmic river of consciousness which bears the healing waters of grace will direct a portion of its flow toward Earth.

But, "No man is an island," as the poet John Donne put it. We are each linked with the consciousness of all mankind. When the general consciousness is low, it is difficult for any man to rise. The great German poet-scientist Goethe, perhaps the greatest mind of his age, attributed most of his genius to the contributions of other minds. No one can rise far above what others before him have already achieved. Thus, when one solitary soul cries out for God, the response—in proportion to the intensity of the call—will not be so great as when a whole community, a whole people call. The spirituality of the one will be diluted, if only somewhat, by the worldliness of the whole.

Yogananda wrote, in his interpretations of the *Bhagavad Gita,* that from time to time in the great storm of *maya,* or delusion, an area of calm appears. There, it is much easier for souls to escape delusion, and find God. He was referring to this same phenomenon: When enough people call sincerely enough, a mighty flow from the river of grace is deflected toward this planet; a new ray of Light is drawn downward, and all who tune in to it are uplifted as they never could be, were they to struggle merely on their own.

Such a call went out in the last century from the Western world, and particularly from the heart of America, in response to the soul-deadening claims of modern materialistic thought. Refined spirits rebelled at the arrogance of scientists who insisted on a mechanistic view of reality. Yet the scientific approach had already proved itself more valid than the dogmatic. Spirituality seemed to be in retreat. What was the answer? Obviously, it was for a divine ray to shine down and offer to spiritualize science itself!

America especially seemed destined to draw this divine ray. Founded as it was on principles of religious freedom, this country, despite its notorious materialism, has always hungered for spiritual truths also. It was onto this soil, accordingly, that the ray shone, through the life and mission of that great master of yoga science, Paramhansa Yogananda.

Few people realize the magnitude of this blessing for this country, and for this age. By the power of this ray, "millions,"

Yogananda said, "will find God." But they only will find Him through this ray who understand what a blessing it offers them, and who take full advantage of it.

Who, then, will say, "But how do I find such a ray?" The prayer has already gone out. It has been answered! Blind ones! Do you not *see* what you have?

A few years ago, while addressing a crowd of about a thousand spiritual seekers in Vancouver, I asked for a show of hands of those who had read *Autobiography of a Yogi.* About seventy-five percent of my audience raised their hands. Yet I doubt that more than ten persons, out of all those present, were devotees of this path.

In Melbourne, Australia, in 1980 I asked the same question of a crowd of two hundred. *Everyone* raised his hand! Yet, once again, the number of devotees of this path of Self-Realization cannot have been more than a handful.

People read *Autobiography of a Yogi* and think, "I must spiritualize my life." And the next thing you find them doing is seeking "soul-awakening" through wheat grass, or raw foods. Or they go to India, and hope to find there another divine ray — not considering that whatever ray they find has been sent to answer the needs of another culture, and another people.

I don't mean to imply that *any* of the things people take up to improve themselves is wrong. But, again, don't they see what they *have*?

I have always felt a distaste for sectarianism. Paramhansa Yogananda himself often said that his work was not a sect. But it is not sectarian to point to the clear blessings that are at hand. When the sun is shining brightly, will an intelligent person decline to benefit from it with the excuse, "Oh, there are other suns in the galaxy!"

True, not all seekers are attuned to this particular ray. It is for each one to decide which ray is best for him. But for every individual whose natural attunement is to another ray, there will be many in our times, and in America particularly, for whose benefit this ray was quite literally heaven-sent.

Transmitting Stations

Common among religious works in the West is the belief that the individual doesn't really count; that what matters is the work itself. Institutionalism has been both the genius and the special curse of religion in the Western world. The genius, because it has offered people clarity and coherency; the curse, because it has said to them, "Unless you accept every definition of truth as we give it to you, you will be damned forever."

The divine ray, however, has no outward form, though it may indeed work through form. As Jesus put it, "The wind bloweth where it listeth . . : so is everyone that is born of the Spirit." (John 3:8) Religious institutions are a blessing only when they offer their teachings in love and freedom; never when they threaten and command.

Truth, to be sure—and as I said earlier—cannot be personalized. It exists even if *no* individuals appear to declare it. Nevertheless, in the spread of a religious teaching "transmitting stations" are necessary. Without people to radiate outward the light they receive in themselves, the light itself dies out in the world. God works through living instruments. This is a teaching that has been insisted on in India.

The individual devotee grows spiritually according to how well he attunes himself to the special divine ray to which he has been drawn. And an important aspect of this attunement is *service* to the ray.

I am thinking particularly of two examples on this path: one, a devotee who for years meditated long hours every day, but who never sensed the need for attunement with the ray represented by his guru; the other, a devotee who for as many years never meditated well, but who served this ray lovingly. I would never downplay the importance of meditation. It is, however, an interesting fact that of the two, the second devotee was by far the more shining.

I'm thinking of another example as well: someone who left Ananda Village, giving up the opportunity he had had for years there to serve the ray actively, in order to live near one of the communities founded by Master and to become absorbed, albeit passively, in those holy vibrations. A year later I saw him again. To my deep regret, he seemed to have lost much of his former spiritual power.

"The instrument is blessed by that which flows through it." As Yogananda said also, "To be in tune with the guru, you must serve his work."

The best way of serving the guru's work is to be, oneself, a transmitting station for the ray of light that his work represents. This one can be whether or not one ever teaches, or, for that matter, even speaks. It is a matter of consciousness: of radiating outward—not only to other people, but to the flowers and trees; to one's work; to the very atmosphere!—the blessings one has received.

For yourself, too, if you want to be more in tune with the ray that is shining through this work of Self-Realization, seek out those who are already in tune with it. I have seen over the years that those who sought their attunement with Yogananda, but who didn't also recognize the need for personal contact with living instruments of his ray, have not received nearly as much.

I remember Master, even when he was alive, telling new disciples to mix more with the older ones. Devotees generally who think to advance on their own, or only in direct inner relationship to Master, don't know what they have in the opportunity to be with others more advanced on the path than they themselves are—those who are *living* instruments of the ray.

A New Movement

The time has come to start a movement among the spiritual seekers of this age. Not all will feel inspired to follow this ray in an institutional sense. But what of it? Paramhansa Yogananda stressed the *inwardness,* as well as the non-dogmatic nature, of his mission. "'Dye them in the wool' of their own divine experience through Kriya Yoga," he used to say, in answer to the "dyed-in-the-wool" dogmatism of so many Christian sects. Through too much dogmatism, divine truth in the West has become suffocated. This is no longer the age of institutionalism, but of individual, inner commitment: of *Self*-realization.

Does any of my statements seem erroneous? And would you like to challenge it? Then please do one thing: Don't ask yourself, "What *should* work?" And don't go on from there to tell yourself: "It must work, so therefore it does!" Rather, look about you and see what *is* working. Base your understanding on what you actually see.

And what should you look for? Those who live in tune with the divine ray will manifest in their lives increased love, harmony, and joy. More especially, they will radiate those particular qualities which belong to that ray. But those who work against the ray will manifest in their lives a growing disharmony, and diminution of love.

An Invitation

Would you like to join this family of Self-Realization? If so, how can you do so?

There are several ways. And in any case, your first step should be to do so in your own heart.

It is possible, first, to limit your joining to a purely inward commitment. But I've already mentioned that those who seek attunement on their own receive less, usually, than those who affiliate with others on the path—particularly with those more advanced. I've stressed also the importance of serving the ray—a thing more difficult, though still possible, to do on one's own.

Why not, then, stress for everyone the importance of outward affiliation?

The reason is that people are constituted differently. Much is lost in religion when everyone is pushed and squeezed into the same mold. Much more is lost when people are threatened, or dealt with angrily, simply because they won't fit the mold. For two thousand years Christian churches have threatened dissidents with eternal hellfire. Nowadays, with the spreading belief in reincarnation, people are threatened with incarnations of future suffering. I myself have been told I would be reborn crippled and blind, merely because I didn't toe someone else's line!

I would offer you this advice, then: Go where you find inspiration. If you follow this simple guideline, and *continue* to follow it whenever the directions change, your attunement will continue to deepen.

Ignore, therefore, the negative reasons why you should not affiliate with others. But there are still, as I've pointed out already, positive reasons why you *should* do so, if you feel so inspired.

Chapter 8

BECOMING A DISCIPLE OF PARAMHANSA YOGANANDA

Those who are seeking to realize God understand the need for a true guru to guide them through the many challenges of life.

Through attunement to a Guru and through God's grace, the disciple's life can be transformed. Referring to the Ananda line God-realized Masters, or Gurus, Paramhansa Yogananda said, "Through the power of this divine ray, millions will find God."

You can learn about Ananda's line of God-realized Masters in Yogananda's *Autobiography of a Yogi*. Our line includes Mahavatar Babaji, Jesus Christ, Lahiri Mahasaya, Swami Sri Yukteswar, and Paramhansa Yogananda. Because of Babaji's prior incarnation as Krishna, Yogananda often referred to him as "Babaji-Krishna".

The guru-disciple relationship is a sacred and eternal bond. To indicate our commitment of discipleship to Paramhansa Yogananda and the line of ourGurus, we take a Discipleship Vow, which is a part of a Discipleship Ceremony.

The Discipleship Ceremony

The Discipleship ceremony is very simple. Ideally it is performed with an Ananda minister, but can also be done at home. You can perform the ceremony by following the instructions below, or you can email **kriyayoga2@ananda.org** for information on downloading a sound file of the ceremony being led by an Ananda minister.

Here is how you can perform this simple ceremony by yourself or with another disciple of Yogananda. Please take the time beforehand to read and fully understand the discipleship vow.

How to Begin

Find a quiet place where you can be undisturbed: your meditation room or another quiet part of thehome. Prepare an altar with photos of the Gurus, and a candle and incense if desired.

Please Have Ready

Flower
Donation in an envelope

The flower symbolizes your devotion to God and our line of God-realized Masters. The donation symbolizes your desire to share their teachings and blessings with others.

Feel free to invite a close friend or another disciple to witness your vow.

You are now ready to begin your Discipleship Ceremony.

DISCIPLESHIP INITIATION CEREMONY

Opening Prayer and Meditation

Begin by mentally (or out loud) praying to Paramhansa Yogananda and the line of God-realized Gurus . Pray thus, or substitute with your own heart-felt words:

Heavenly Father, Divine Mother, Friend
Beloved God, Jesus Christ, Babaji-Krishna, Lahiri
Mahasaya, Swami Sri Yukteswar, Paramhansa
Yogananda, I bow to you all.

Divine Mother, bless me that I might attune my life to Thee and to this divine line of Gurus that you have sent to me. Help me to understand the true meaning of discipleship. Bless me that I may follow my divine teachers until I reach Self-realization.
AUM, Peace, Amen.

Chant if you like, then meditate briefly, attuning yourself to Divine Mother and the line of God-realized Masters.

Prayer

Repeat silently

Heavenly Father, Divine Mother, Friend Beloved God, Jesus Christ, Babaji-Krishna, Lahiri Mahasaya, Swami Sri Yukteswar, Paramhansa Yogananda, I bow to you all.

Divine Mother, I come before Thee today having long sought Thy eternal light, long pondered the eternal truths, long followed the winding path that leads to Thee.

I have walked with my own strength, all too seldom with Thine. I have walked with the thought, "I want this from life; these answers; that guidance; this pathway, or that," but I have seen that, as often as I made claims onlife, it eluded me. As often as I presumed on Thy will, it turned away from me.

Ah, too long, Mother, have I sought Thee for myself,not for Thy love. I know now that, without Thy strength added to mine, infusing it, I shall never find Thee. Thine is the power, the grace, the infinite glory.

With loving faith now I seek Thee Through the ray of Thy light that Thou hast offered me. I will ascend to Thee not by my power alone, but by the power of Thy infinite love. I am Thine, Mother, be Thou eternally mine.

Vow of Discipleship

Repeat out loud

I offer myself in service and devotion to Your cause, and to the ray of the divine light as it is represented by Your channels, Jesus Christ, Babaji-Krishna, Lahiri Mahasaya, Swami Sri Yukteswar and Paramhansa Yogananda.

Accept me into this family of Self-Realization, and make me also, through them, an instrument of Thy blessings. Thus, as I receive, may others be blessed also to receive.

I will join my energies to those of my gurubhais, my spiritual family on earth.

I will cooperate with them, and especially with the living representatives and guides of my divine line of Gurus.

Discipline me, guide me, purify me. Teach me to attune myself to Thy ray, until at last, through daily meditation, service and devotion I unite my soul with Thy Infinite Spirit.

Offering

Kneel before the altar and silently pray to the line of Gurus, placing your offerings of the flower and donation on the altar.

Closing Prayer

Heavenly Father, Divine Mother, Friend Beloved God, Jesus Christ, Babaji-Krishna, Lahiri Mahasaya, Swami Sri Yukteswar, Paramhansa Yogananda, I bow to you all.

Divine Mother, Thank you for your many blessings. May Thy love shine forever on the sanctuary of my devotion, and may I be able to awaken Thy love in all hearts. I am Thine. Be Thou eternally mine.

AUM, Peace, Amen.

Donation

The donation, which symbolizes your desire to help share the teachings of the Gurus with others, can be sent to Ananda at the address below. It will be used by Ananda Sangha for spreading Yogananda's teachings. Please include a note stating that it represents your Discipleship donation.

Address
Ananda Sangha
14618 Tyler Foote Rd.
Nevada City, CA 95959

Appendix

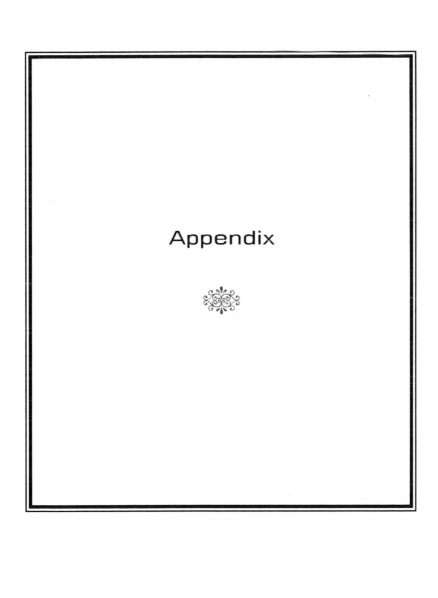

Kriya Yoga is a meditation technique that quickly accelerates one's spiritual growth. It was first made widely known by Paramhansa Yogananda in his *Autobiography of a Yogi*. According to Yogananda, Kriya is the most effective technique available to mankind today for reaching the goal of *Yoga*: union with the Divine.

Yogananda taught Kriya Yoga as part of a spiritual path that includes three other techniques, along with discipleship to the Kriya line of God-realized Masters. The Kriya technique itself is not mechanical in the way that it works. It is effective only to the extent that the Kriya yogi practices it with awareness, sensitivity, devotion, and in conjunction with other practices taught by Yogananda.

Ananda teaches the four techniques that encompass the Path of Kriya, just as Yogananda taught them:

• Energization Exercises

• *Hong Sau* technique of concentration

• AUM technique of meditation

• Kriya Yoga technique

The first three are taught in the different steps of the Ananda Course in Self-Realization. The Kriya technique is given through personal initiation, and only after establishing a regular daily practice of the first three techniques. This process takes about a year or more, depending on the student.

Students can also study these materials through Ananda Online Classes at **www.anandaonline-classes.org** or through an Ananda teaching center. If one studies through the Ananda Course, the following steps lead to initiation into Kriya Yoga. For purchase of materials please see the *Resources Section*.

Step 1 *Lessons in Meditation*

Learn the basic techniques of meditation through clear, step-by-step instructions. Experience the importance of the breath/mind connection and the power of the focused mind. Learn also Paramhansa Yogananda's energization exercises, which teach a little-understood secret of success: gaining conscious awareness of and control over your energy.

This course offers techniques that are part of the path of Kriya Yoga, including the *Hong Sau* technique of concentration. There are also many simple, "do-able" suggestions, such as how to sit comfortably for meditation, how to still the restless mind, and how to take your experiences of peace and joy into daily life. Included with the illustrated book is the Companion Audio CD with guided meditations, visualization, and the Energization Exercises DVD demonstrating the energization exercises.

Step 2 *The Art and Science of Raja Yoga*

The most comprehensive guide on yoga and meditation offered today. It gives us the balanced and complete approach of raja yoga, which is also known as the "royal" yoga. This guide is organized around seven topics: Philosophy, Meditation, Postures, Breathing, Routines, Healing Principles and Techniques, and Diet. It also includes in-depth discussions of the paths of karma, bhakti, and gyana yoga. The author, Swami Kriyananda, excels in showing the interdependence of these seemingly separate areas and how all of them, when correctly approached, further our spiritual progress.

Course support contact information: course@ananda.org, 530-470-2340

Step 3 *A Handbook on Discipleship*

Swami Kriyananda (J. Donald Walters) shares insights into the importance and practice of the Guru/Disciple relationship. Stories of his personal experiences with Paramhansa Yogananda help to prepare the student for either an at-home or in-person initiation into discipleship to Yogananda and to the line of Masters of Self-Realization, if he or she feels ready for this level of commitment.

Step 4 *Kriya Yoga Preparation*

The Kriya Preparation book includes instructions in the AUM technique of meditation and further prepares the student for Kriya Yoga initiation. This book is available with permission from the Ananda Kriya Sangha after completion of the other parts of the Ananda Course, and completion of the ceremony of discipleship mentioned above.

Step 5 *Kriya Yoga*

Kriya Yoga is a technique that is part of the path of Kriya Yoga, as taught by Paramhansa Yogananda. It is given through initiation, after completion of the entire Ananda Course, and establishing a regular daily spiritual practice using the main techniques that are part of the path of Kriya. Application to receive initiation into Kriya can be made to:

Kriya Sangha contact information:
email: kriyayoga2@ananda.org
phone: 530-478-7624
mail: Ananda Kriya Yoga
14618 Tyler-Foote Road,
Nevada City, CA 95959

Spiritual Roots

The *Ananda Course in Self-Realization* is based on the teachings of Paramhansa Yogananda, author of the spiritual classic *Autobiography of a Yogi.* Yogananda was the first great Indian master of yoga to make his home in the West. By sharing with countless Americans the life-transforming techniques of yoga and meditation, he opened the door to their own direct experience of spiritual realities.

● ● ● ● ● ● ● ●

Paramhansa Yogananda

"As a bright light shining in the midst of darkness, so was Yogananda's presence in this world. Such a great soul comes on earth only rarely, when there is a real need among men."

—The Shankaracharya of Kanchipuram

Paramhansa Yogananda was born in India in 1893. He was trained from his early years to bring India's ancient science of Self-realization to the West. In 1920 he moved to the United States to begin what was to develop into a worldwide work touching millions of lives. Americans were hungry for India's spiritual teachings, and for the liberating techniques of yoga.

In 1946 he published what has become a spiritual classic and one of the best-loved books of the twentieth century, *Autobiography of a Yogi*. In addition, Yogananda established headquarters for a worldwide work, wrote a number of books and study courses, gave lectures to thousands in most major cities across the United States, wrote music and poetry, and trained disciples. He was invited to the White House by Calvin Coolidge, and he initiated Mahatma Gandhi into Kriya Yoga, his most advanced meditation technique.

Yogananda's message to the West highlighted the unity of all religions, and the importance of love for God combined with scientific techniques of meditation.

"Swami Kriyananda is a man of wisdom and compassion in action, truly one of the leading lights in the spiritual world today."
—Lama Surya Das, Dzogchen Center, author of *Awakening The Buddha Within*

SWAMI KRIYANANDA

A prolific author, accomplished composer, playwright, and artist, and a world-renowned spiritual teacher, Swami Kriyananda refers to himself simply as "a humble disciple" of the great God-realized master, Paramhansa Yogananda. He met his guru at the young age of twenty-two, and served him during the last four years of the Master's life. And he has done so continuously ever since.

Kriyananda was born in Rumania of American parents, and educated in Europe, England, and the United States. Philosophically and artistically inclined from youth, he soon came to question life's meaning and society's values. During a period of intense inward reflection, he discovered Yogananda's *Autobiography of a Yogi*, and immediately traveled three thousand miles from New York to California to meet the Master, who accepted him as a monastic disciple. Yogananda appointed him as the head of the monastery, authorized him to teach in his name and to give initiation into Kriya Yoga, and entrusted him with the missions of writing and developing what he called "world-brotherhood colonies."

Recognized as the "father of the spiritual communities movement" in the United States, Swami Kriyananda founded the Ananda World Brotherhood Community in the Sierra Nevada Foothills of Northern California in 1968. It has served as a model for seven communities founded subsequently in the United States, Europe, and India.

In 2003 Swami Kriyananda, then in his seventy-eighth year, moved to India with a small international group of disciples, to dedicate his remaining years to making his guru's teachings better known. He appears daily on Indian national television with his program *A Way of Awakening*. He has established Ananda Sangha Publications, which publishes many of his one hundred literary works and spreads the teachings of Kriya Yoga throughout India. His vision for the next years includes founding cooperative spiritual communities in India (there are two communites now in India, one in Gurgaon and the other in Pune); a temple of all religions dedicated to Paramhansa Yogananda; a retreat center; a school system; a monastery; as well as a university-level Yoga Institute of Living Wisdom.

Ananda Sangha Worldwide

Ananda Sangha is a fellowship of kindred souls following the teachings of Paramhansa Yogananda. The Sangha embraces the search for higher consciousness through the practice of meditation, and through the ideal of service to others in their quest for Self-realization. Approximately ten thousand spiritual seekers are affiliated with Ananda Sangha throughout the world.

Founded in 1968 by Swami Kriyananda, a direct disciple of Paramhansa Yogananda, Ananda includes seven communities in the United States, Europe, and in India. Worldwide, about one thousand devotees live in these spiritual communities, which are based on Yogananda's ideals of "plain living and high thinking."

Swami Kriyananda lived with his guru during the last four years of the Master's life, and continued to serve his organization for another ten years, bringing the teachings of Kriya Yoga and Self-realization to audiences in the United States, Europe, Australia, and, from 1958–1962, India. In 1968, together with a small group of close friends and students, he founded the first "world-brotherhood community" in the foothills of the Sierra Nevada Mountains in northeastern California. Initially a meditation retreat center located on sixty-seven acres of forested land, Ananda World-Brotherhood Community today encompasses one thousand acres where about 250 people live a dynamic, fulfilling life based on the principles and practices of spiritual, mental, and physical development, cooperation, respect, and divine friendship.

At this time, after forty years of existence, Ananda is one of the most successful networks of intentional communities in the world. Urban communities have been developed in Palo Alto and Sacramento, California; Portland, Oregon; and Seattle, Washington. In Europe, near Assisi, Italy, a spiritual retreat and community was established in 1983, where today nearly one hundred residents from eight countries live. In Pune and Gurgaon, India there are two communities and a spiritual retreat center.

The Expanding Light

We are visited by over two thousand people each year. Offering a varied, year-round schedule of classes and workshops on yoga, meditation, spiritual practices, yoga teacher training, meditation teacher training, and personal renewal retreats, the Expanding Light welcomes seekers from all backgrounds. Here you will find a loving, accepting environment, ideal for personal growth and spiritual renewal.

We strive to create an ideal relaxing and supportive environment for people to explore their own spiritual growth. We share the nonsectarian meditation practices and yoga philosophy of Paramhansa Yogananda and his direct disciple, Ananda's founder, Swami Kriyananda. Yogananda called his path "Self-realization," and our goal is to help our guests tune in to their own higher Selves.

Kriya Support: kriyayoga@ananda.org • 530-478-7624

Guests at The Expanding Light can learn the four practices that comprise Yogananda's teachings of Kriya Yoga: the Energization Exercises, the *Hong Sau* technique of concentration, the AUM technique, and Kriya Yoga. The first two techniques are available for all guests; the second two are available to those interested in pursuing this path more deeply.

Ananda Sangha Contact Information
mail: 14618 Tyler Foote Rd., Nevada City, CA 95959
phone: 530-478-7560
online: www.ananda.org
email: sanghainfo@ananda.org

Expanding Light Contact Information
mail: 14618 Tyler Foote Rd., Nevada City, CA 95959
phone: 800-346-5350
online: www.expandinglight.org
email: info@expandinglight.org

Resources

Books

Published by Crystal Clarity Publishers

**Crystal Clarity publishes
the original 1946, unedited edition of
Paramhansa Yogananda's spiritual masterpiece**

Autobiography of a Yogi
by Paramhansa Yogananda

This edition, featuring previously unavailable material, of a true spiritual classic, *Autobiography of a Yogi*: one of the best-selling Eastern philosophy titles of all-time, with millions of copies sold, named one of the best and most influential books of the twentieth century.

This highly prized verbatim reprinting of the original 1946 edition is the ONLY one available free from textual changes made after Yogananda's death. Yogananda was the first yoga master of India whose mission was to live and teach in the West. His first-hand account of his life experiences includes childhood revelations, stories of his visits to saints and masters in India, and long-secret teachings of Self-realization that he made available to the Western reader.

The New Path

My Life with Paramhansa Yogananda
Swami Kriyananda

The New Path tells the story of a young American's spiritual quest, his discovery of the powerful classic, *Autobiography of a Yogi*, and his subsequent meeting with—and acceptance as a disciple by—the book's author, the great spiritual teacher and yoga master, Paramhansa Yogananda.

Swami Kriyananda is an extraordinary narrator: He recreates the vibrancy of his guru's presence, remembers Yogananda's words with perfect clarity, and communicates to the reader the depth of their meaning. Through Kriyananda's eyes and words, you'll be transported into Yogananda's immediate presence as you learn the highest yogic teachings.

The New Path provides a marvelous sequel to Paramhansa Yogananda's own *Autobiography of a Yogi*, helping you to gain a more profound understanding of this great world teacher. Through hundreds of stories of life with Yogananda and through Swami Kriyananda's invaluable insights, you'll discover the inner path that leads to soul-freedom and lasting happiness.

WHAT OTHERS ARE SAYING ABOUT THESE GREAT WORKS:

"*Reading* Autobiography of a Yogi *by Paramhansa Yogananda was a transformative experience for me and for millions of others. In* The New Path, *Swami Kriyananda carries on this great tradition. Highly recommended.*"
— Dean Ornish, M.D., Founder and President, Preventive Medicine Research Institute, Clinical Professor of Medicine, University of California, San Francisco, author of *The Spectrum*

"*Swami Kriyananda has written a compelling and insightful account of his own life, as well as revealing his remembrances of Paramhansa Yogananda.* Completely revised and updated, The New Path *is filled with profound reflections, insights, experiences, challenges, and spiritual wisdom. Required reading for every spiritual seeker. I heartily recommend it.*"
— Michael Toms, Founder, New Dimensions Media, and author of *True Work* and *An Open Life: Joseph Campbell in Conversation with Michael Toms*

"*[T]he teachings, the message, and the life of Paramhansa Yogananda are illuminated in a way that makes it possible for us to not only easily access his timeless wisdom, but—through the elegantly easy-to-follow explanations and the living example of one of Master's most devoted disciples—actually apply Eternal Truth to our present-day life. It is impossible for me to think of a greater gift that humanity could receive at this critical time in our evolution as a species, and I am personally and forever grateful to Swamiji for this blessed offering.*"
— Neale Donald Walsch, author of *Conversations with God*

Energization Exercises Practice Aids

DVD: On track one, Barbara Bingham presents the exercises with detailed instruction. On track two, Swami Kriyananda leads the exercises before a class.

Wall poster: with the complete descriptions and illustrations.

Guided Audio CD: for those that need an audio reminder on how to do these exercises. Track one has a detailed description of the exercises. Track two is in a "call-out" style of each exercise name to help you through the complete set.

More Titles to Serve You on The Path to Kriya Yoga

The Essence of Self-Realization: The Wisdom of Paramhansa Yogananda, Recorded, Compiled, and Edited by Swami Kriyananda. Nearly three hundred sayings rich with spiritual wisdom, explaining life's true purpose and the way to achieve that purpose.

Whispers from Eternity: Paramhansa Yogananda, Edited by His Disciple Swami Kriyananda. Yogananda's beautiful prayer-poems draw God into all aspects of daily life. A non-sectarian devotional scripture that honors God in all forms, pointing us to the universal inner experience of Self-Realization.

How to Meditate, by Jyotish Novak. A clear and concise guidebook that explains the essential techniques to meditation.

Meditation for Starters, by Swami Kriyananda. A simple book providing what you need to begin a meditation practice.

Awaken to Superconsciousness: How to Use Meditation for Inner Peace, Intuitive Guidance, and Greater Awareness, by Swami Kriyananda. A clearly written guide to raising one's awareness out of ordinary consciousness into superconsciousness.

Audiobooks, Music, & DVDs

Crystal Clarity's complete catalog of music and audiobook titles are available through our website or from any of the popular online sources.

AUDIOBOOKS

Meditation for Starters, by Swami Kriyananda. A guided meditation and visualization.

Metaphysical Meditations, by Swami Kriyananda. Thirteen guided meditations, based on the mystical poetry of Yogananda, set to a background of well-known and inspiring classical music

MUSIC

Chanting CDs performed by Ananda Kirtan, using harmonium, guitar, tablas, kirtals, and done in a live kirtan style. The titles include:

Bliss Chants	Divine Mother Chants
Power Chants	Peace Chants
Love Chants	Wisdom Chants
Wellness Chants	

Mantra CDs chanted by Swami Kriyananda.
AUM: Mantra of Eternity
Gayatri Mantra
Mahamrityanjaya Mantra
Maha Mantra

DVDs
Yoga for Busy People, by Gyandev McCord and Lisa Powers
Yoga to Awaken the Chakras, by Gyandev McCord
Yoga for Emotional Health, by Lisa Powers

Retreat Centers

The Expanding Light
14618 Tyler Foote Road, Nevada City, CA 95959
800-346-5350
www.expandinglight.org

Ananda Seclusion Retreat
14618 Tyler Foote Road, Nevada City, CA 95959
530-292-3024
www.meditationretreat.org

Ananda Online Courses

The Ananda Course in Slef-Realization can also be done
online, with additional material such as video and audio talks.

www.anandaonlineclasses.org

Crystal Clarity Publishers

When you're seeking a book on practical spiritual living, you want to know it's based on an authentic tradition of timeless teachings, and that it resonates with integrity. This is the goal of Crystal Clarity Publishers: to offer you books of practical wisdom filled with true spiritual principles that have not only been tested through the ages, but also through personal experience.

We publish only books that combine creative thinking, universal principles, and a timeless message. Crystal Clarity books will open doors to help you discover more fulfillment and joy by living and acting from the center of peace within you.

Crystal Clarity Publishers—recognized worldwide for its bestselling, original, unaltered edition of Paramhansa Yogananda's classic *Autobiography of a Yogi*—offers many additional resources to assist you in your spiritual journey, including over one hundred books, a wide variety of inspirational and relaxation music composed by Swami Kriyananda, Yogananda's direct disciple, and yoga and meditation DVDs.

For our complete online catalog, with secure ordering, please visit us on the web at:

www.crystalclarity.com

Crystal Clarity music, spoken word, and audiobooks are available for download on the popular online sites.

To request a catalog, place an order for the products you read about in the Further Explorations section of this book, or to find out more information about us and our products, please contact us:

Contact Information

mail: 14618 Tyler Foote Rd., Nevada City, CA 95959
phone: 800-424-1055 or 530-478-7600
online: www.crystalclarity.com
email: clarity@crystalclarity.com

CPSIA information can be obtained at www.ICGtesting.com
Printed in the USA
BVOW021900180213

313586BV00001B/2/P